Incredible Customer Service

INCREDIBLE CUSTOMER SERVICE

The final test

David Freemantle

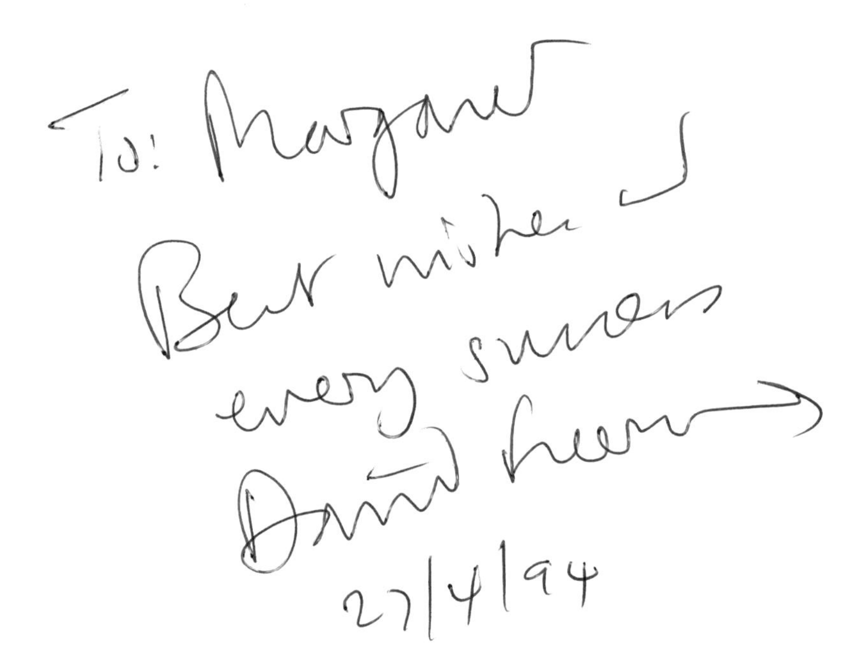

McGRAW-HILL BOOK COMPANY

London · New York · St Louis · San Francisco · Auckland
Bogotá · Caracas · Lisbon · Madrid · Mexico
Milan · Montreal · New Delhi · Panama · Paris · San Juan
São Paulo · Singapore · Sydney · Tokyo · Toronto

Published by
McGRAW-HILL Book Company Europe
Shoppenhangers Road, Maidenhead, Berkshire, SL6 2QL, England
Telephone 0628 23432
Fax 0628 770224

British Library Cataloguing in Publication Data
Freemantle, David
Incredible Customer Service: Final Test.–
New ed
I. Title
658.812

ISBN 0-07-709008-X

Library of Congress Cataloging-in-Publication Data
Freemantle, David.
Incredible customer service / David Freemantle.
p. cm.
ISBN 07-709008-X
1. Customer service. 2. Customer service—Case studies.
I. Title.
HF5415.5.F727 1992
658.8′12—dc20 92-25429

1 2 3 CUP 9 6 5 4

Typeset by BookEns Limited, Baldock, Herts
and printed and bound in Great Britain at the University Press, Cambridge

Dedication

To:
Mechi
who came from so far away
to give so much love

Acknowledgements

This book would not have been possible without the help of a large number of people whose contribution I really appreciate.

Firstly, over the last few years a large number of participants on my seminars have contributed stories about their experiences of customer service, both good and bad. I have meticulously taken notes of what they have said and furthermore I have taken the liberty of quoting many of their stories in this book. I am thankful for all these inputs.

Secondly, I appreciate the time given to me by a number of people who helped me with the research for this book. These include Alex Templer, Director of BMW, Altwood of Maidenhead; Cedric Brown, Managing Director of British Gas; Dr Marvin H Goldberg, Chairman of AMI Healthcare; Richard Barker, Operations Director of Waterstone's Booksellers; Alan Breakwell, Chief Executive of East Dorset District Council; D Bruce Pattullo, Governor of the Bank of Scotland; Ernie Hughes, Personnel Executive of Cornhill Insurance; Roger Burrell, Director of Customer Service with ICL; Nigel Davis, Managing Director and Eric Jones, Director of Service and Repair at H&C Ltd. I am also indebted to Miles Kington of *The Independent* newspaper for giving me permission to reprint an article by him.

Thirdly, I would like to thank Kate Allen of McGraw-Hill who encouraged me to write this book and has provided valuable advice in the preparation of it. Her support has been constant.

Finally, I would like to thank my wife Mechi who, being

Venezuelan, does not have English as her first language but is a far better proofreader than any English person I've come across. She has made an important contribution to this book.

Contents

Introduction

'Customer service is the final test. You can get everything else right, in terms of product, price and marketing, but unless you complete the process with incredibly good customer service you run the risk of losing business or even going out of business'.

Over the last few years some organizations have taken tremendous strides forward in providing incredibly high standards of service to their customers. For example back in the early eighties British Airways had a dreadful reputation for customer service. Today they provide a level of service that is among the best, if not the best, in the airline industry. BMW is another company which excels in an industry not generally renowned for high quality customer service.

These examples, together with a few others, are rare within the general experience of customers who frequently have to suffer the disinterest and inefficiency of companies who fail to deliver the goods on time, who make little effort to reduce waiting times or improve telephone responses. Perhaps the most common experience when trying to secure service is encountering staff who lack a positive, warm and friendly disposition towards the customer.

The surprising thing is that the concept of customer service is not new, in fact it has been on the lips of most managers in most industries for the last decade or two. But perhaps that is where it has remained, on the lips but not in action. Customer service, in fact, has been given a lot of lip through expensive training programmes and parades of certificates of the people who have attended them, through posters and exhortations and even through declarations of intent to customers. Yet, in practice, the success rate has been poor. Too many organizations have yet to get the simplest aspects of customer service right – for example, getting through on the telephone quickly, or answering letters promptly, or getting a service engineer to arrive punctually.

The most galling aspect of all this is that many companies profess, through their advertisements and publicity to provide service par excellence, yet consistently fail to live up to their words.

Car dealers, airlines, hotels and public utility companies have all jumped on the bandwagon – but often to little real effect. Frequently the service the customer experiences is totally divorced from the 'service excellence' image these companies try to project. It is almost as if the company has done no more than devise a clever service slogan and left it at that – for all to see – but never to be acted upon.

For many, both within an organization and customers of it, the idea of customer service has become a bit of sham, a bit of a gimmick. It has become a superficial and fashionable phrase which in practice has little meaning. In fact the term 'customer service' is used as a bureaucratic cosmetic in a superficial attempt to hide the ugly cracks in the way the company treats its customers.

This book explores the reasons why so many companies fail to live up to their words. It is based on two fundamental assumptions:

1. That customer service is all about getting some basic things right;
2. That the process of getting them right is all to do with good management.

There is nothing magical or clever about customer service, it is in fact very basic. The problem is that too many companies have ignored these basics, concentrating their energies on product, marketing and financial performance at the expense of the customer. Customer service should be a fundamental and integral aspect of any business and should be given equal weight in strategic considerations about the company's future. In fact, as customers acquire more disposable income during the 1990s, their criterion of choice will rely less on product and price but more on service. With the increasing availability of modern technology, companies will find it relatively easy to compete on product. What they will find more difficult to do is compete on service, for service not only depends on modern technology but also on the attitude of its people and therefore the capability of its managers.

Customer service is a concept that is applicable to all industries and organizations and all their employees. It is not a concept that should be confined to front-line people who have to serve in shops, hotels, restaurants and airlines. Customer service is equally applicable to personnel people serving the line, to finance departments serving the organization and also to senior executives who have to service their companies with a high degree of leadership support and direction. Furthermore customer service has direct relevance to public sector organizations as well as commercial firms. Local councils, government agencies, the National Health Service and the police force all have much to gain by developing their approach to customer service (and many have).

The first part of this book spells out 14 key components of the 'final test'. These 14 tests of customer service are applicable to all companies and organizations, whether they be in the private or public sector. The tests are immutable and reflect the very basics of customer service. For example, you can talk about customer service as much as you like, but unless you can achieve a five second telephone response time you haven't even got the basics right. The basics are represented by these 14 key tests, any organization which passes them all will have achieved an incredible standard of service potentially unrivalled by any of its competitors. In fact, the 14 tests presented here could well be integrated into an organization's 'Customer Service Charter' – now that the 'charter' concept is becoming increasingly popular.

The second part of this book looks at how you can manage to pass this final test and thereby achieve an *incredible customer service*. The focus is on a simple no-nonsense, common-sense, pragmatic approach to management. As with customer service, there is nothing magical or clever about management, it is all to do with getting the basics right and the second part of this book spells out those basics of management needed to achieve great success in customer service.

At the end of each chapter, there are a number of personal challenges for you, the reader, in your attempt to achieve superb customer service. The implication is that you can take some steps today to improve customer service in your own area of responsibility. Part Three summarizes some of these practical steps. None of them require massive injections of resource or capital; all they require is some of your time and a positive attitude towards serving the customer.

The final section of this book presents some brief case studies of organizations that have excelled at customer service over recent times. The case studies used illustrate the basic principles covered in the previous parts. Also included are one or two (anonymous) examples of organizations providing exceptionally poor service.

Scattered throughout the book are a number of 'Stories customers tell . . .' which illustrate the points being made. All these stories are true and have been provided by participants on the author's 'Customer Service' workshops. To avoid embarrassment, the author has avoided naming those organizations providing poor service.

Overall, the book is aimed at stimulating you to consider whether you can pass the final test of business success and what action you might need to take in relation to this.

'LOW PRIORITY' GIVEN TO CUSTOMER SERVICE

'Improvements in customer service and product quality are a low priority for top executives of privatised companies, according to a survey out yesterday.

'Of the 33 companies privatised since 1979, 36 chairmen and chief executives and 16 from a further 13 organisations still in the public sector, were surveyed. Up to 81 per cent said they were most concerned about managing a corporate culture change.

'Asked to name their priorities, only 27 per cent of the executives were personally concerned about product quality, while only 18 per cent highlighted customer service.'

Independent, 12 October 1990

Part 1

THE 14 KEY TESTS OF CUSTOMER SERVICE

'There are 14 key tests for incredible customer service. These tests are very basic and applicable to all types of organizations whatever sector of industry, commerce or public service they are in. In fact they reflect the fundamental core of all exceptional customer service.'

You can philosophize for ever about customer service, but unless you and your organization strive to pass these tests you will never make any progress. Those organizations that focus on the attainment of the standards represented by these tests are those which will succeed during the next decade.

These standards are immutable in that they are timeless, virtually irreducible and of universal application. There are additional standards (and therefore tests) which might well be specific to the type of business you are in, but while these are important they will not be dealt with in this part of the book. Further reference to these industry-specific standards is made in Chapter 18.

THE 14 KEY TESTS FOR INCREDIBLE CUSTOMER SERVICE

1. **Keeping the service promise**
2. **Five second telephone responses**
3. **Documentation responses within two days**
4. **Five minute maximum waiting time**
5. **Positive employee attitudes**
6. **Proactive communications**
7. **Honesty and openness**
8. **Systems reliability**
9. **Swift reparation**
10. **Being in the know**
11. **Front-line ownership**
12. **Little extras**
13. **Attention to detail**
14. **Immaculate appearance**

This first part of the book considers each one of these key tests.

Test 1

Keeping the service promise

'All declarations of intent made by the organization, corporately or by individual employees and thus perceived by customers as promises must be met.'

As soon as you let a customer down you lose business.

Companies win business by promising service and retain business by keeping this promise.

- They promise to deliver within seven days and do so.
- They promise to get a service engineer to your broken-down machine within eight hours of calling and do so.
- They promise to reply within two days and do so.
- They promise to call back this afternoon and do so.
- They promise to replace a defective product immediately with no questions asked and do so.
- They promise a fast, efficient, friendly service and prove it with a charm and courtesy that is rare today.
- They promise that the machine will work, will be reliable, and it is.

Keeping the service promise is such a basic test that it is both surprising and frustrating that so many organizations fail to pass it.

Keeping the service promise should be an absolute priority for any manager intent on achieving success on the customer service front.

Some personal challenges

- Do you go out of your way to make promises to your customers?
- Do you go out of your way to keep all the promises you make, whether minor or major?
- Are you aware of the promises your team makes and whether or not they consistently keep them?
- Do you seek independent feedback that the promises you and your team make are always kept?

There is no point in reading on unless you can honestly answer 'yes' to the four questions above. If the answer is 'no' to any one of them you need to take urgent personal action to address the situation.

Your own personal credibility is at stake when you fail to make promises and fail to deliver on them.

REMEMBER:
The more promises you and your team make, the more you keep and the better the service!

THE STORIES CUSTOMERS TELL . . .

AIRLINE - FINE WORDS, POOR SEATS

'I booked an expensive holiday in Florida for our honeymoon. I rang the airline a few days before we departed to try to reserve two seats together. They told me seats would be allocated on check-in but assured me there would be no problem in getting two together. On the day of travel we arrived at the airport at the time they told us to, only to find long queues at check-in. When we got to the desk we were told the flight was virtually full and that I couldn't sit next to my wife.'

TELEPHONE INSTALLATION - GERMANY

'I was assigned to a post in Munich and after a brief spell in a hotel I moved into a new apartment. Because of my work I needed a telephone installed fairly quickly. I applied to the telephone company and by return of post I received a card saying their engineer would arrive between 9.45am and 10.15am the following Monday to install the phone, please could I arrange to be in. Believe it or not the engineer arrived promptly at 10.00am. As a result I had minimal time off work. It took my breath away as you would never get this sort of response in Britain.'

LOCAL BUILDER - POOR AFTER SALES SERVICE

'We moved to Berkshire a year ago. We like the house and generally it was well built. But there have been a whole succession of minor defects which have meant a constant stream of telephone calls to the builder's after-sales department. I have always tried to pin them down to a specific time when the plumber, electrician or repair-person would visit as both my wife and I are very busy and not always in. On each occasion they have given us a time, for example Thursday morning or Monday afternoon. On not one single occasion have they turned up during the designated period. On most occasions it has taken two or three further telephone calls and quite a few more days to get the person to attend. Both my wife and I have wasted so much time waiting in for people who never turn up.'

GARAGES - SUB-STANDARD SERVICE

'Thousands of garages are servicing cars so badly that they are unfit to be on the road, according to a survey in the latest *Which?* magazine. Of 30 garages surveyed only four were rated 'good'. In four garages the mechanic had not removed the wheels - a necessary step to check the brakes . . . One South Wales garage rated as "very poor" . . . left the car with low brake and clutch fluids, no attention for any of the grease points, the sidelight and number plate light not working, a slack fan belt, no lubrication of the door locks and hinges, under-inflated rear and spare tyres, a loose battery terminal and the wheels not removed to check brakes.'

Report, The Independent, 6 September 1990

Test 2

The five second telephone response

'All telephone calls to the organization should be answered within five seconds.'

Every second lost by a customer beyond five seconds waiting for a call to be answered, or lost due to repeated dialling when the line is engaged, will diminish the goodwill and credibility of the organization and eventually result in lost business.

Customers have thresholds. These vary. But as soon as an organization crosses the threshold of too protracted a response to a telephone call, the customer will feel bad and behave accordingly. He or she might take it out on the organization's staff (who will not necessarily be at fault). More likely they might take their business elsewhere.

That threshold is unlikely to be within five seconds. Organizations that really strive for incredible customer service will therefore set as a prime standard a five second telephone response time to all calls.

The standard is applicable to all organizations whether they be travel agents, airlines, theatre booking offices, car dealers, hospitals, doctors' surgeries, town halls or hotels.

No excuse is acceptable. Poor managers always make excuses. They will complain of peak demand and unpeaked resources. They will complain of insufficient capital investment in the organization. They will complain of unpredictable circumstances.

There can be no excuse. An effective telephone response must always be a priority.

For the narrow-minded, cost-conscious financial director, who strives for a mean level of efficiency, it might appear to make sense to cut the number of telephonists from 10 to 8 because 20 per cent of their time is not utilized effectively. But a prospective customer who turns away because he or she cannot get through is an unquantifiable loss which probably exceeds any potential saving.

But it is not just the 'front-line' response time at the switchboard that requires ongoing attention.

It is the response time of every single telephone in the organization. Too often, customers obtain a quick effective response on calling the company, only to be shunted through to an internal telephone that rings forever. This doubles the agony in that the customer is now paying hard-earned money for the ringing telephone.

The five second standard test should therefore apply to every telephone in the establishment. No matter how busy people are, they need to double-check that their telephones are covered at all times and ensure that an effective response is provided whatever the situation.

Answerphones are a solution to the unanswered call but should not be used excessively, especially internally within the organization.

Equally important is a high standard of response in terms of the attitude of the person answering as well as a high quality answer. This will be dealt with in Chapter 5.

Another telephone test which relates to 'keeping the service promise' is that all messages taken over the telephones must be followed up by the person taking the message. It is just not good enough to leave a scrap of paper on a person's desk and assume that the message will be acted upon. Chapter 11 covers this aspect.

You might also consider some additional tests relating to telephone responses, for example ensuring that your staff always give their names when answering calls so that customers know who to contact should some follow-up action be necessary.

Some personal challenges

- When out of your office ring up and ask for yourself from time to time. If the response from your switchboard is consistently longer than five seconds, you must take action to improve the system, whatever your position in the organization. If a slow response alienates you, it could also be alienating your customers (upon whom your own performance and success relies).
- If your own telephone remains unanswered after five seconds then that is your own personal failure. If it happens consistently you should be fired! How can any customer deal with you?
- Take remedial action before you get fired. If they fail to fire you, your organization is going to go out of business eventually and you will lose your job anyway!

REMEMBER:

The telephone is often the first and frequently the last point of contact a customer will have with your business!

THE STORIES CUSTOMERS TELL . . .

ELECTRIC IRON MANUFACTURER - FOUR DAYS TO GET THROUGH

'We saw a notice in our newspaper that the cable on our new iron was potentially dangerous and that we should ring a given number between 8.00am and 10.00pm for advice. Well, we tried for four days. I suppose we made between 40 and 50 attempts to get through from early in the morning to late in the evening. It wasn't until the fifth day that we got through. I mentioned the problem of trying to get through but they didn't seem interested.'

LOCAL COUNCIL - 'IT'S NOT *MY* PHONE RINGING'

'I'll tell you how bad some of the people in this council are. Amongst other things I manage the council's switchboard. One lunch time the police rang through to say they had a potential suicide case on their other line. The person had given her name but no other information. Could we check her name out with Social Services to see if they could provide any relevant information. The telephonist rang through to Social Services upstairs but got no response, the line just kept ringing and ringing. After three minutes the telephonist left the switchboard and raced upstairs to the Social Services Department. She found three social workers drinking coffee there and chatting away. Nobody else was around. Nearby on someone else's desk the telephone was ringing, it was the call the operator had tried to put through. "Why don't you answer the phone?" the operator asked. One of the social workers shrugged her shoulders. "That's not our phone," one of the others answered, "anyway it's our lunch hour." I wrote a letter of complaint to the Director of Social Services, so did the Police. We got a very negative and defensive reply back.'

CAR SERVICE - CAN'T GET THROUGH ON PHONE

'I bought this executive car from a local dealer. The problem was that whenever I went to book it in for service I could never get through. The switchboard answered alright, but the phone just seemed to ring and ring in service reception. On one occasion I rang for ten minutes before giving up.'

Test 3

Documentation responses within two days

'All documents from customers requiring a response should be acknowledged within two days and specify a final date for a completed response.'

Many documents from customers don't require responses, like payments for invoices, personal information updates, completed questionnaires.

Many other documents do: applications for services, letters of enquiry, comments about the organization. There is no good reason why these and many others should not be acknowledged, by letter, telephone, or by personal action within two days. If further action is required beyond the two days (for example, investigating a complaint, researching an enquiry), then a final date for completed action should be given.

The achievement of this simple standard will reduce the need for customers to chase issues, as well as reducing wasted time for staff who are distracted by having to look into these issues.

A related test of *incredible customer service* is that 'the person to whom the document is addressed will personally respond to the enquiry.' This standard also comes under the heading of 'Front-line ownership' in Chapter 11.

You should never invite the customer to write to the Chief Executive unless the Chief Executive is personally prepared to reply. Equally unsolicited letters to the Chief Executive must always be replied to and signed by the Chief Executive, whether they number one or a thousand a week. If there are a thousand a week then the organization has a major customer service problem, which the Chief Executive needs to address.

In addition to ensuring a response within two days by the appropriate person, it is equally important to ensure that the quality of the response is of the highest possible standard.

Customers' names must be spelt correctly, initials used where given and titles applied appropriately. Addresses and other relevant facts must be recorded and stated precisely. Invariably, the tone of the document must be courteous, helpful and presented in a 'customer-friendly' way.

Word-processed responses to personal letters alienate. Standard letters should also be avoided when the enquiry is personal. Customer service is all about building up long-standing relationships and when the customer writes in about a unique problem (unique in his or her eyes), he or she deserves a unique reply which will help cement the relationship. Standard word-processed letters should be reserved for mass communications applicable to all customers.

Some personal challenges

- Sit down with all your people, together with copies of a complete set of documents that have been sent from your department to customers (internal or external) over the last week.
- Together, constructively criticize these documents in terms of:
  - Speed of response
  - Method of response
  - Quality of response
  - Who was accountable for the response.

- Don't be frightened to 'pin-prick' and find fault in an aspect. Blame yourself (not your staff) for any short-coming.
- Ensure that every single member of your staff is aware of and trained to achieve the high standards of documentation and document response time required to serve your customers exceptionally well.

REMEMBER:
A quick courteous response to a letter saves time, creates goodwill and is a thousand times more profitable than any delay!

THE STORIES CUSTOMERS TELL . . .

FAST RESPONSE FROM COUNCIL - SLOW RESPONSE FROM BUILDERS

'I had this problem when our neighbours installed a temporary dwelling in their garden - virtually underneath our bedroom window. This mobile home was to house a number of visitors from overseas. I raised the issue with the neighbour (who we hardly ever saw) and his reaction was "The dwelling will be gone in a few weeks time when the visitors depart. If you don't like it sue us."

'I wrote to the local council complaining that this dwelling contravened planning control and building regulations. The council wrote back the same day explaining the action they were taking. Four days later the dwelling had been removed.

'I also wrote to the developers of the estate who were the lessors, as the temporary dwelling contravened the leasing agreement. It took them six weeks to reply!'

CUSTOMER HOT LINE - GONE COLD

'I bought this small portable computer. There were certain aspects of its operation I didn't understand. In a newsletter sent with the computer was a hot-line number to ring if customers had problems. I rang the hot-line and was answered by an answer-phone. I left a message explaining my problem and asked them to call me back on the number I gave them. A day later there had been no call-back. So I rang again and left a second message on the answerphone. Again there was no response. Four days later I wrote to the company complaining about the lack of response. What was the point of advertising a hot-line number if it didn't work? That was months ago. They never replied to my letter. Yet they still send me mailshots advertising upgrades, additional facilities and other features I may well want to buy. But no way!'

COUNCIL RESPONSE TIME REDUCED FROM SIX WEEKS TO TWO DAYS

'In our land searches section we have reduced the response time on enquiries from an average of about six weeks to an average of two days. We have done this without a massive investment in computerization, but by using a more pro-active approach and ensuring that information is immediately available when requested.'

Council Officer, London Borough of Enfield

Test 4

Five minute maximum waiting time

'In no circumstances should any customer have to wait more than five minutes for service.'

I hear the cries already: 'Impossible'; 'He lives in an unreal world, a fantasy land'.

Other more progressive managers will proclaim that five minutes is too long and the standard should be two minutes. Those banks, hotels, retail stores, travel companies and organizations which pass this five minute test will gain my custom and the custom of many more.

Some supermarket chains and some hotel groups are virtually achieving this standard. Others fail lamentably, as in the case of many High Street post offices.

Time is money. Customers waste valuable time and money by having to wait for service. Companies investing time and money in minimizing wait-times and striving for a maximum five minute standard will gain much custom. It can be achieved, and there are a number of measures which can help:

1. **Flexibility of resources**
   Adequate reserves of trained people should be available to be deployed to the front-line at a moment's notice, to alleviate

queueing problems and reduce waiting times. This requires the elimination of demarcation barriers, the broadening of job descriptions and investment in training.

2. **A roving eye (the 'queue buster')**
   One person (a 'queue buster' with a 'roving eye') should be assigned accountability for monitoring customer waiting times and taking immediate action to minimize them by opening up more service delivery points.

3. **A constant study of waiting patterns**
   Believe it or not, most peaks and troughs of customer demand fall into patterns which can be analysed and planned for. In other words, most demand-peaks are predictable. Sophisticated computer techniques are available to help analyse waiting time data and predict demand. Resourcing and administration (teabreaks etc.) can be planned accordingly.

4. **Appointments**
   Where customer transactions are protracted, an appointments system should be established. This should not be confined solely to the provision of professional services. It might be preferable for a retail outlet to offer the facility of an appointment for the potential purchase of an expensive item (a carpet, a kitchen or a bedroom suite) rather than have a customer with £10,000 in his or her pocket go elsewhere because no sales-person is available in the showroom.

5. **Sensitivity and courtesy**
   Front-line staff should be sensitive to customers queueing behind the person they are currently serving. A smile and a comment such as 'I'll be with you as quickly as I can' to anyone they see waiting will go a long way to appease frustrated customers.

Those organizations that believe that their customers will always be prepared to wait a long time because they have always done so, will have a rude awakening. A reduction in waiting times means a greater throughput of customers, better productivity and increased revenue.

By choice, customers will always turn to the company that doesn't keep them waiting. By choice, customers will always discover who has the shorter queues.

Some personal challenges

- Check out the times your department's customers have to wait for service. Are you really happy with these times? Do they exceed the five minute test? Is this really what you want for your customers?
- Remember that this test is equally applicable to internal customers, for example staff queueing in canteens, at the cashiers, in the clinic and elsewhere in the company.
- If you have queues, time them and establish a pattern for different times of the day. How far are you away from passing the five minute test?
- What can you do about achieving the five minute standard?

REMEMBER:

It doesn't necessarily require a massive injection of resource to reduce waiting times, sometimes a healthy dose of imagination in using existing resources more flexibly will solve the problem.

THE STORIES CUSTOMERS TELL . . .

BANK - OPENING TILLS TO RELIEVE QUEUES

'I always keep an eye on what's happening out front. As soon as I see a queue forming I'll get someone to open up an extra till to relieve the congestion'.

Assistant Branch Manager, Lloyds Bank

LUNCH TIME QUEUES AT BANK

'The only time I can get to my bank is at lunchtime. I invariably encounter a lengthy queue alongside the ropes. Sometimes the queue is outside the door. On many occasions I've had to queue for twenty minutes.

'What really frustrates me is that they actually reduce the number of tills open at lunchtime. Apparently they send their staff to lunch then! It's like going to a restaurant and being told "We can't serve you lunch because the waiting staff are having their own break".

'The first bank that cracks the lunchtime queue problem will have my business!'

SUPERMARKET - LESS QUEUEING - MORE BUSINESS

'We had shopped at the same supermarket for over thirty years. I supposed we had become accustomed to having to queue for up to twenty minutes to go through checkout on Friday evenings or Saturday mornings. We never questioned why we had to queue, we just took it for normal. Then Tesco's opened a new superstore nearby and we tried that out. We were amazed to discover that we didn't have to queue - even at these busy times. We always go to Tesco's now and it's very rare we have to wait. I discussed this with my mother and discovered she's also switched to Tesco's where she lives. And it's the same with my brother too! It seems that our whole family has switched their allegiance!'

FIVE HOUR WAIT - HOSPITAL OUTPATIENTS

'I had to take my mother to the hospital for a 10.15am appointment. We arrived at 10.00am and reported to reception. We waited in a crowded room until 3.00pm. I couldn't leave her to get some tea, just in case we got called. I kept on enquiring when we might be seen but the receptionist was very unhelpful.'

SLOW RESTAURANT SERVICE

'It's one hotel I will never go to again. Every time I went there the service was so slow I almost went beserk. Last time, after we finished our main course, we stared at our dirty plates for over half-an-hour before we could get them removed. The waitresses seemed to be in a mad rush all the time and studiously avoided our eyes. In the end I had to go and get the duty manager to get some service.'

Test 5

Positive employee attitudes

'Every single interaction between a customer and a representative of the organization will be conducted in a courteous, friendly and positive way with a genuine show of interest for the customer.'

There is no doubt that one per cent of customers behave in the most atrocious way. They expect the impossible and put extreme pressures on highly-stressed, front-line staff.

This one per cent is not representative of the 99 per cent of customers who are both tolerant and reasonable and who expect to be treated in a caring fashion but who frequently are not.

With sensitive and courteous handling even the one per cent can become reasonable.

Positive employee attitudes are reflected in the simple things of life: a warm smile, a friendly word, a genuine display of interest, a sensitive glance, a welcome piece of unsolicited information, a thank you. These are amongst the little courtesies of life. They have a magical effect on customers, and yet there is nothing magic about them.

All the sins of a defective support organization can be forgiven by a customer, with the repair of a warm smile and real initiative used by a front-line person. Spilt coffee, excessive delays, faulty articles, wrongly despatched goods and so on can rapidly be redeemed by staff who take positive action to rectify the mistakes, who treat the customer with sincere compassion, heart-felt interest and decent accord.

Believe it or not, it doesn't take much to please most customers. Conversely, it often takes a lot to alienate a customer. Customers are extraordinarily forgiving if not extraordinarily appreciative of any positive attitude displayed by an employee. It is absolutely astounding that so few organizations recognize this and therefore fail to encourage such attitudes.

This simple test of customer service is readily measurable. You only have to ask your customers how they feel about your front-line staff and the attitudes they display.

Some personal challenges

- Examine your own attitudes. When was the last time you went out of your way to please a customer (internal or external)?
- How do you gauge the attitude shown by your people to your customers? Do you really know that it's positive?
- How aware are you of your customers' reaction to your people?
- How do you assess the opportunities for improving such attitudes?
- Why not initiate a 'courtesy' campaign towards your customers? You will need to discuss with your team what 'courtesy' really means.

REMEMBER:
A positive attitude must emanate from you!

THE STORIES CUSTOMERS TELL . . .

SHOE SHOP - GOING OUT OF THE WAY

'I saw these shoes in the window at Manfield's which I liked. The assistant was very helpful. Unfortunately they didn't have my size. The assistant rang around other branches in neighbouring towns and eventually discovered a pair in my size. I collected them the next day. I always go there now and they always recognize me, call me by name, enquire after my kids, sometimes give me coffee.'

RESTAURANT - TOTAL DISINTEREST

'We decided to have dinner before the concert in the concert hall's own restaurant. We nearly missed the concert, despite arriving for dinner 90 minutes beforehand. They got our order wrong and only served two out of the three main courses we had ordered. The food was served in a very sloppy way, the salad was limp and stale, the salmon burnt. They brought us the wrong wine. No attempt was made to offer us coffee and we had to chase that. Overall, the staff didn't seem interested in serving us. Everybody seemed passive and reactive. On the table was a customer comment card. I completed it, writing down what I thought and leaving my name and address with a request that the manager write to me. I never did get a reply.'

HOTEL - FAULTLESS SERVICE

'I ran a conference at the Forte Hotel at Aylesbury. The staff really put themselves out to make sure everything was alright. The service was faultless, there was always someone around to help. Hotel staff were always popping in to ask "Is everything okay, is there anything I can get you?" '

HITLER AT DOCTOR'S RECEPTION

'It's like getting past Hitler to get past the receptionists at my doctor's.'

SUPERMARKET - VOLUNTEERING TO HELP

'I went to the new Tesco's superstore at Slough and bought two trolley loads of groceries. Not only did I get through the checkout in record time - and it was Friday evening, but the checkout lad arranged for someone to pack for me. The lady who packed then volunteered to help me wheel the two trolleys out to the car park. She then adamantly refused my tip!'

POSITIVE POLICE

'My father, who is 70, came to visit us from Ireland. At the end of his stay, we put him on the train at Slough to connect at Reading for Fishguard. He's done the journey many times and normally rings us when he arrives home. On this occasion we heard nothing. So we rang my aunt. He had not arrived. We began to get worried. We rang British Rail and they confirmed the train had arrived on time in Fishguard. We rang the ferry company and apparently the ferry had sailed for Rosslare on time. So we notified the police at Slough. They were incredibly helpful, they really put themselves out. They came round and took a description. They in turn notified the Irish police and they all set about searching for my father. They checked at all stations and searched both ferry ports, but my father was not to be found.

A day later, my father rang from home in Ireland. Apparently he had missed his connection at Reading. So he went for a couple of pints, got himself bed and breakfast and then caught the following day's train. He had not rung us because he didn't want us to worry.

I was so embarrassed when I rang the police to tell them. They were so understanding.'

Test 6

Proactive communication

'When things go wrong get to the customer before the customer gets at you.'

Things will go wrong. Sometimes it's *outside* your control (for example, service engineers get delayed on motorways, resources get diverted because of bad weather emergencies). But sometimes it's *within* your control (for example, you underestimated the stock required, you got the address wrong).

Whatever happens, if the service promise to the customer cannot be kept, it is imperative that you inform them before they inform you. This proactive communication test is one that many companies fail to pass. You create goodwill by contacting customers about problems before they find out about them some other way. By the time a customer starts chasing you, he or she feels bad, and will have been alienated to a degree.

By ringing up and explaining the problem, you keep control of the situation, you avert potentially damaging side-effects. Customers will forgive the delay, the short-fall or the error, if you tell them about it first. When they discover it is too late, they will be on the war-path.

Too many people, even today, wait in for goods that are due to arrive, but never do; for service engineers who have promised to come but don't. Nothing is more frustrating than a failure by the company to proactively communicate in such circumstances.

In these days of the car phone, mobile phones, phone cards, fax machines and couriers, there is absolutely no excuse for a failure to communicate when things go wrong.

Even when things are going right, goodwill will be gained when your staff take the initiative to communicate with the customer, to inform him or her that everything is in hand, that progress is being made, that things will happen when they say it will happen.

Furthermore, goodwill is created simply by contacting a customer and asking how things are going, whether they are satisfied with the product or service.

Some personal challenges

- Look at your service delivery records. On those occasions where you or your team have fallen short, do you know for a fact that action has been taken to communicate with the customer beforehand?
- Talk to your customers when there has been a service problem. Are they happy with the level of communication provided?
- Talk to your people. Are you confident they go out of their way to keep their customers informed?
- Re-read the correspondence with your customers. Does this give you any indication of how good or bad you are at proactive communications?

REMEMBER:

When the customer reacts, it's often too late, far better that you speak first and take action accordingly.

THE STORIES CUSTOMERS TELL . . .

UNHELPFUL AIRLINE STAFF

'Our flight was delayed by three hours at Heathrow. I was with my wife and two kids. I went to the airline desk when I discovered the delay and asked about refreshments. They were unhelpful and gave me no indication I was entitled to free refreshments. Then by accident, as I was queuing up to buy a snack for my family I discovered that the man in front of me had free meal vouchers from the same airline. The cashier got me to show our boarding passes and told me we could spend up to five pounds each at the airline's expense. The airline hadn't bothered to tell me anything about this, in fact had indicated the reverse.'

'SHE RARELY ANSWERS A SERVICE CALL BECAUSE HE RARELY HAS TO MAKE ONE.'

Caption above a photograph of a stewardess serving a passenger in Delta Airlines advert:

'Observation.
A skill all Delta Airlines stewardesses are trained in.
They can often see when you want that extra pillow. Or maybe some more coffee.'

HOSPITAL DRAGON

'My son gashed his leg badly. I bandaged it as best I could and took him to the outpatients at our local hospital nearby. The lady on reception was a real dragon. She took our details and told us to wait. There were hundreds of others waiting too, screaming kids, old people looking as if they were about to die.

'We waited for three and a half hours before a doctor attended to us. During that time nobody told us how long it would be before our turn. We tried to ask, but the dragon just told us to sit down and wait.

'They must have known it would be a long wait. If only they had told us we could have done something, gone for a coffee or to buy a paper to pass the time.'

FRIDGE FIASCO

'I bought this fridge and was told it would be delivered Saturday. By 5.00pm Saturday it hadn't arrived. Thinking the showroom would shut at 5.30pm I rang up. I was told it was on the van. It didn't turn up. I rang again at 6.30pm but of course the showroom was by now shut. I rang Monday and was told it would be delivered that morning. It wasn't. I stayed in all day. I rang at 2.00pm and couldn't get through. At 3.00pm I rang again and spoke to another person who said they didn't deliver on Mondays, only Tuesdays and Thursdays. I got cross at this point and that made the person at the other end even crosser. Nobody seemed to bother. My wife waited in all day Tuesday. No fridge came. We felt like cancelling the order. Finally the van turned up Thursday. They offloaded the fridge and carted it into our kitchen. When they took the packaging off we discovered it was the wrong model. The driver said he couldn't take it back. I rang up again and after a few days chasing they delivered a second fridge. Now we had two fridges, the right one in our hallway and the wrong one in our kitchen. The driver refused to take the first fridge back as he had no instruction to do so and it would get in the way of the other drops he had to make. After four weeks we eventually got the problem sorted. Not once did anyone ring us, or apologize, or take any initiative to sort the problem out. We were constantly on the phone trying to get things fixed.'

Test 7

Honesty and openness

'All communications from the organization to the customer must be on a completely open and honest basis. Nothing should be hidden from the customer nor should there be any variations on the truth (half-truths, excuses, distortions, white lies).'

It is not that companies are blatantly dishonest – it is just that sometimes they are 'economical with truth' or 'distort the facts'. Such is the famous 'small print' of life – things you really want the customer to overlook, to neglect, to ignore.

When you sell a product or service it seems logical to present it in the very best light, to stress its positive points. After all, that's what sells.

Conversely, it would seem totally illogical to mention a product's weaknesses, limitations, defects and shortcomings in the sales literature and during the sales pitch. So a lack of openness is bred into the system of buying and selling.

The same applies to customer service. It is a struggle to tell the truth when things go wrong, especially when there has been a high degree of incompetence or miscommunication, resulting in massive inconvenience to a customer. But tell the truth you must. It is one of the key tests of customer service.

In being honest and open with the customer, you don't have to give value judgements about your colleagues (who might have let you down) – but you can report the facts, for example:

- A message wasn't passed on;
- The address was incorrectly recorded;
- Two of the staff are new and don't yet know the system;
- The wrong serial number was given to the warehouse;
- We had you down as 'out' Tuesday not 'in';
- The service engineer was sick yesterday;
- You forgot to re-order that stock item.

In selling a product, it is absolutely essential that sales people clearly present the level of aftersales service their customers can reasonably expect – and also mention any restrictions applicable, for example on cancellation charges, refunds or exchange of defective goods.

Honesty and openness also relate to those all important details of customer service, like a promise to phone back, to put a letter in the post, to deliver within a few days. In fact, everything an employee says to a customer must be on an open and honest basis.

Honesty and openness should permeate every facet of customer service.

Some personal challenges

- Be honest with yourself.
- How often do you 'fob off' a customer with some 'half-truth'?
- How often are you expedient by making some weak excuse to the customer?
- How often do you suppress information which might be of vital interest to the customer?

REMEMBER:
'When you hide the truth the customer will ultimately discover it'.

THE STORIES CUSTOMERS TELL . . .

LIFT COMPANY - BEING UPFRONT WITH CUSTOMERS

'We believe in listening to people, to our engineers, to our customers. In fact we liaise very carefully with our customers. We let them know when we're coming, what's going on. We let them know if we encounter any problems, if there are any shortcomings - for example getting behind on our service schedules. Whatever mistake we make - and we occasionally do - we're upfront with our customers.'

Supervisor, Hammond and Champness, Lift engineering company

BANK - SURPRISE FEE

'I rang my bank manager to renew my overdraft facility. He did so willingly. When my statement came later, I discovered an "arrangement fee of £150" for renewing this facility. It was the first time in twenty years they had levied such a charge. What was worse, the bank manager had not mentioned the charge to me when we spoke.'

DISSATISFACTION WITH BUILDING SOCIETIES

'Dissatisfaction with building societies is now growing fast. Complaints to the Building Societies Ombudsman grew by 50 per cent last year to 2,577 and have tripled since 1987. The key break with the past is that societies increasingly discriminate against existing members, in order to attract new ones. Prospective borrowers are offered lower interest rates than current borrowers. Prospective investors are favoured over existing recruits who are (temporarily) locked into obsolete accounts, paying lower rates. Building society chiefs have traditionally dismissed those who complain as old-fashioned fuddy-duddies who hark back to a non-existent golden age of mutuality.'

Report, The Independent on Sunday, 4 August 1991

CAR DEALER - HONESTY PAYS

'We sold this customer a second hand BMW. He soon brought it back complaining of a water leak in the boot. We patched it. A week later he brought it back in with the same problem. This happened a number of times. We kept on patching.

'We asked the body shop to have a real close look. They reported back that this car had been in a major accident and then rebuilt. We hadn't known this when we bought it in and sold it on.

'The body shop reckoned it would need a couple of weeks work done on it. Our policy is to be completely open and honest to the customer. So we explained the problem to the customer. We offered him a replacement car whilst the problem was sorted or he could have his money back. He took his money back. A few weeks later he bought a more expensive car from us.

'Our policy here is to be completely honest with the customer.'

General Manager, BMW Dealership, Maidenhead

BANK - PROFITING AT EXPENSE OF EXISTING CUSTOMERS

'When my bank brought out its new interest bearing account, I never received a mailshot about it, nor an invitation to convert my existing account to this new account. I asked why. The bank's answer was simple "We don't want our existing customers to change from their existing accounts, which are highly profitable for us, to less profitable interest bearing accounts." '

Test 8

Systems reliability

'The service system should fail the customer on no more than one in a thousand occasions.'

Put it another way: the system for providing service to the customer should always work; the television in the hotel room, the cashpoint, the escalator in the department store, the lift at your headquarters, the car park barrier, the record of your reservation or your special request. Regrettably, the system frequently fails, the system which sends out bank statements late, gets personal information incorrect, despatches invoices for goods not ordered or for goods already paid for, the system which consistently fails to ensure you get routine service checks and reminders. Then there are the defective systems which send you the wrong goods, or deliveries which are short, or the same delivery twice.

Systems neglect is endemic. Who ensures that the system works? Who ensures that the radiator in the conference suite is functioning properly, that the information sent to the customer is up-to-date, that the wake-up call comes, that the goods are correctly priced and labelled before being put on the shelves, that invoices get paid within 30 days, that the refund cheque is actually attached to the letter?

Why is it that so many organizations seem to have run out of exactly what you need when you ask for it and can never seem to get anything right?

There should be a system for everything relating to the customer: a system for ensuring that the basic service is delivered effectively and efficiently; a system for ensuring that immediate action is taken when any aspect of the service fails; a system for ensuring that feedback from customers and the requests they make are acted upon; a system for ensuring that promises made by one employee are acted upon by others; a system for ensuring there is effective ongoing communication with the customer; a system for ensuring that all information about customers is accurate and up-to-date.

There are those rare organizations where everything runs smoothly, where the customers feel that everything is under control, that everything works virtually all the time – and when something occasionally does go wrong it is fixed quickly and efficiently. These are the organizations that deliver on time, whose documents always contain accurate information. These are the organizations that put a high degree of emphasis on and achieve exceptionally high standards of systems reliability.

Some personal challenges

- Do a test run. Get some of your friends and neighbours to test your organization's customer service systems and report back to you objectively. Any costs they incur should be charged to the company.
- How long it takes them to get paid for the costs they incur will be an excellent test of the service system.

REMEMBER:
'A systems failure is no more than a management failure.'

THE STORIES CUSTOMERS TELL . . .

'We changed our address and sent out almost 500 notes to that effect. You would be amazed how many companies still send correspondence to our old address.'

'I was away on business and stayed at this hotel just outside Glasgow. I ate alone in the restaurant that evening. The main course was inedible so I sent it back. The waiter offered me an alternative but I declined suggesting that he make a deduction from my bill. The waiter consulted the head waiter who agreed to the reduction. After the meal I ordered decaffeinated coffee. They told me they had run out. I went without. The second evening of my stay I went again to the same hotel restaurant. The food was somewhat better. I asked for decaffeinated coffee again. They told me they had run out. Now opposite the hotel was a little grocer. How is it that no one had bothered to go and purchase some decaffeinated coffee?

'When I went to check out the following morning, I found that my bill had not been adjusted as previously agreed. The cashier wouldn't take my word for it when I asked for the reduction and insisted on consulting the head waiter. But he was on a different shift and had gone home. It took ten minutes and the duty manager to get my reduction sorted out.'

'I ordered this book by mail order. After six weeks it hadn't come. I rang the company. It came four days later. The invoice came quickly too. I paid immediately. A week later, a second copy of the same book arrived. I also received an invoice for the two books. I had not ordered a second copy. I wrote a letter asking for a postage prepaid label to return the second book. They wrote back saying they didn't have such labels but they would refund the postage and packing costs as soon as I returned the second book. I returned the book and sent a separate letter with a note of the postage and packing costs. Two weeks later I received a further invoice showing I had paid for the first book but owed them money for the second book I'd already sent back. I ignored the invoice. My refund for postage did not come. Four weeks later I received a letter threatening legal action if I did not pay for the second book. I wrote a letter of complaint asking for a refund and objecting to the continued invoicing. Four weeks later I received an apology and a cheque for five pounds.'

'The invoice payments procedure for the council completely broke down at one stage. The results were horrific. Bakers who had not been paid refused to supply bread to residential homes, nor could we get simple subcontracting work done. In one incident, a minibus taking a group of elderly people on a day trip was driven to a local garage to be filled up with petrol. The garage refused to supply the petrol because its account had not been paid by the council. It was a hot summer's day. Those poor old people were left sitting in the bus for over an hour whilst the driver sorted out the problem.'

'I am sitting in a lonely hotel room writing this. It is the depth of winter. The radiator is incredibly noisy and it seems it will gurgle all night long to stop me sleeping. The toilet does not flush properly, the toilet roll is running out and there is no spare. There is an inadequate supply of milk with the tea and coffee making facilities. Breakfast doesn't start till 7.30am and I need to be away by 7.45am . . .

THE NEXT MORNING . . .

'. . . The token they gave me to open the car park barrier after checking out failed to lift the barrier. I have driven very close to the machine in order to drop my token in. I struggle through the nine inches of space between the car door and the barrier and borrow the token from the driver waiting patiently behind me. His token doesn't work either. We lose twenty minutes getting a maintenance person to let us out of the hotel car park.'

Test 9

Swift reparation

'Immediate action must be taken, without hesitation, to redress any product defect or shortfall in service to the customer.'

We have not quite made it to paradise yet. Despite our frequent rage, we have to tolerate the imperfections of our fellow human beings (in the same way I suspect that they have to tolerate us).

What is intolerable is the 'second order' failure to make swift reparation for a 'first order' mistake. Most of us will tolerate the mistake if it is openly and honestly admitted and early action is taken to redress it.

As soon as a company hesitates in redressing a problem with a customer, a critical alienation will occur. Conversely, swift reparation can produce a perception of a higher standard of customer service than if the problem had not occurred in the first instance.

Too many customers experience 'drag' in resolving their problems. Such 'drag' can occur for a variety of reasons:

- Front-line staff lack initiative and other essential skills.
- Front-line staff have insufficient powers delegated to them (in other words there are too many bureaucratic and financial constraints).
- Lack of trust in the customer.
- Incredibly poor management.

As soon as 'drag' begins, the customer will become cynical about the company's intent, believing that once the purchase has taken place no one really bothers thereafter.

Things will go wrong, it is inevitable. A key test of *incredible customer service*, therefore, is that all staff are trained to take immediate remedial action to solve any customer problem they happen upon.

Management support is essential in achieving this, for immediate remedial action often means diverting oneself from assigned pre-planned priorities. It can mean committing unbudgeted expenditure and – if the rules haven't caught up – breaking the rules. These management aspects will be dealt with in Part 2.

Some personal challenges

- List all the customer service problems, minor or major, you and your team have encountered over the last week or two. (If you cannot do so you are not customer-oriented.)
- Taking for granted you've been addressing the major problems, focus your attention now on the minor problems. What have you done to address them?
- Has it ever occurred to you that a minor problem for you might be a major problem for a customer?
- Has it ever occurred to you how much business you lose by a failure to address these niggling little problems of customer service?

REMEMBER:

'There are no minor problems of customer service.'

THE STORIES CUSTOMERS TELL . . .

DEFECTIVE FRIDGE - IMMEDIATE REPLACEMENT

'I bought this fridge. When they delivered and unpacked it, I found it was scratched all down one side. The delivery men had no hesitation. They took it away and brought back a replacement the same day.'

COUNCIL - TWO AND A HALF YEARS OF ARGUING

'A few months after I moved into this council flat I found part of the wall in the kitchen was getting wet. I wanted to redecorate and put some tiles up, but couldn't. So I rang the council's housing department. It took me days to get through. They said they would send someone round to look at it. No one came. I chased and chased - it cost me a lot in telephone calls. After two months, someone came to look. He said the plumbing had been installed incorrectly, that one of the pipes was leaking. He would put it down as an emergency job. It took another two months for the plumber to come. He did some soldering and told me I'd have to wait a few months for the wall to dry out. Well I waited. The wall never seemed to dry up - in fact it got worse. A year passed and I complained again. I'm sure my health was being affected - I suffer a lot from sore throats. They came and resoldered in the end. And then I had to wait again. I asked about getting the wall replastered (it had been alright when I moved in) but they told me I would have to claim that on my insurance. It's now two and a half years since the problem occurred and I'm still arguing with the council.'

PUBLIC UTILITIES - MONTHS TO GET OVERPAYMENT REPAID

'I have this budget account with a public utilities company. I found they were charging me too much. It took me two months and innumerable calls to get my money back. They blamed it on the computer. When finally I did get a cheque it had the wrong name on it!'

AIRLINE - EXCELLENT AT REDRESSING MISTAKES

'The reason we have such a high reputation for customer service is that we are always making mistakes. Our planes are frequently late, we even spill coffee over passengers from time to time. What we excel at is the action we take to overcome these problems. We have so much practice you see!'

British Caledonian, Cabin Staff Stewardess, 1982

Test 10

Being in the know

'All employees should be in the "know":
- ***Know the product;***
- ***Know the service;***
- ***Know the organization;***
- ***Know how to get things done;***
- ***Know how to get problems resolved;***
- ***Know regular customers by their name.'***

Ignorance is far from bliss when the customer fails to get an answer, fails to receive sensible advice, fails to elicit a meaningful response.

Ignorance in front of customers is commonplace. For example it exists when:

- Employees do not know their stock;
- Employees do not know the price or how to determine it;
- Employees do not know how it works;
- Employees do not know the basic features of the product or the service provided;
- Employees do not know who's who in the organization;
- Employees do not know the procedure for resolving a problem.

An important aim of customer service must therefore be to encourage and enable all employees to acquire as much knowledge and experience as possible in order to deal with any customer enquiry or eventuality.

Such knowledge bestows confidence on the customer as well as the employees. It engenders total belief in the company. Employees will feel valuable as they develop increasing degrees of expertise and the customers will be reassured by the degree of confidence exhibited by the employees.

Helping employees gain that all important knowledge to assist customers effectively is an exciting challenge both for managers and employees.

Some personal challenges

- Run a regular 'Being in the know' quiz for the people in your organization and award prizes for the winners.
- Get your people to test you too.

REMEMBER:

The only way your customers can know that you are the best is when your people are 'in the know'.

THE STORIES CUSTOMERS TELL . . .

HOTEL - CHANGES FOR THE WORSE

'I'd stayed at this hotel many times over the last two years. Everyone seemed to know me - for example at reception when I checked in they always greeted me by name, always made sure I got my favourite room. They even knew which newspaper I wanted and the usual time for my wakeup call. In the restaurant, they knew I liked a table with plenty of light so I could read, they knew I liked vegetarian food and a simple apple for dessert followed by decaffeinated coffee.

'Then things began to change. There were new staff who didn't recognize me and knew nothing about me. They didn't seem to know I was a long-standing and loyal customer. I went to have a chat with the manager who was also new. He proudly told me he'd had to fire quite a few of the previous staff who were apparently quite unprofessional.'

COMPUTER ACCESSORY - NO KNOWLEDGE OF IT

'I phoned up this computer services company to order a radiation screen for my computer. Although the product was in their catalogue the sales assistant at the other end knew very little about it. She couldn't tell me delivery times, she couldn't tell me how the screen would fit to the computer - or even whether it would fit. She couldn't even confirm the price in the catalogue.'

HOTEL - BREAKFAST TIME?

'On checking in at reception, I enquired about the time breakfast was served the next morning. I was told 7.30am. I thought I would double-check with the porter who took my bags to the room. He told me 7.00am. When I checked back with receptionist they confirmed 7.30am. When I went down to breakfast at 7.30am the next morning I found quite a few guests already half-way through their breakfast. Apparently the restaurant opened at 7.00am.'

ELECTRONIC TYPEWRITER - HOW DOES IT WORK?

'When I set up my business I needed to buy an electronic typewriter. I went to a major retailer in the High Street and saw the very machine I wanted. The trouble was there was no assistant around to help me purchase it. Eventually I found a young lady and asked if it was possible to give me a demonstration. She told me she didn't know how the machine worked. At this stage I gave up. Later, I looked in Yellow Pages for a dealer who specialized in this make and found one. I went to his shop, he spent an hour demonstrating the same typewriter to me and then sold it to me for £60 less than I would have paid in the High Street.'

Test 11

Front-line ownership

'The person who interfaces directly with a customer must be able and willing (without fear of recrimination from management) to respond effectively to a customer and therefore have the discretion to make a decision in that customer's favour, whatever the circumstance.'

There is nothing more frustrating than the sorts of response that go like this:

- 'I'm afraid I can't authorize this, I'll have to get approval . . .'
- 'I can't deal with this, I'll put you through to . . .' (and then you're kept hanging on);
- 'I'll have to speak to . . . about this';
- 'It's nothing to do with me, you'd better ask . . .';

Some poor customers are shunted from one person to another in the organization, perhaps having to explain a complicated problem three or four times over.

An important test of customer service is that whoever the customer happens to speak to must take direct responsibility for ensuring that that customer is dealt with satisfactorily. Switchboard operators should ensure that callers get a response by checking back on the line. Receptionists must take responsibility for people waiting in their area. Sales assistants must be able to resolve their customer queries and complaints, for example replacing defective goods and making refunds. People on customer service desks must always be able to make decisions on behalf of their customers.

As soon as the front-line starts 'shunting' problems back into the organization's interior, customers will lose patience. Their time will be wasted, they will feel distrusted.

The shunt can occur for a number of reasons:

- Front-line staff are not trusted to make decisions;
- There are inadequate front-line procedures or systems for dealing with customer enquiries and problems;
- Front-line staff have too narrow a definition of their job and are not trained to take a broader 'total' view of customer service;
- Once the sale is made nobody is really bothered about the customer;
- There is a lack of 'corporateness' – of departments not working together, or one department having a different set of 'customer' priorities than another. Consequently, one department can often let another down (manufacturing fails to deliver on a sales promise).

Achieving front-line ownership is therefore all to do with people-management. It is to do with recruiting people who can be trusted, who can take initiative, who have a positive attitude towards the customer. It is to do with training. It is also to do with everyone feeling part of a corporate entity rather than parochially relating to one department only. Ultimately, it is to do with senior management's attitude towards their front-line employees and customers.

Some personal challenges

- Look critically at all the customer interfaces in your department and re-examine the types of decision your front-line people can make when in contact with customers;
- Check also that your front-line people have sufficient information to provide sensible responses to customers – and do not constantly have to be referring elsewhere for basic data;
- Look critically at the decisions your supervisors, managers and you yourself make in relation to your customers and try to delegate as many of these as possible to your front-line people;
- Be honest, do you really trust your front-line staff to make the sorts of decisions you can personally make? If the answer is no, you had better sit down with your team and treat this as an urgent problem. If you don't trust your people, your customers will be suffering and you will be losing business!
- Be honest, how corporate are you? Are you prepared to help out other departments in their quest for customer satisfaction. Do you encourage your people to demonstrate that 'corporate' ownership as opposed to a narrow parochial 'departmental' ownership?

REMEMBER:
Whatever you own your people can own!

THE STORIES CUSTOMERS TELL . . .

CREDIT CARD QUERY - IMMEDIATE RESPONSE

'I had a query about one of the items on my credit card statement. I rang up, the phone was answered in three seconds and the person answering it dealt with my query. I had expected to get shunted through to another department.'

CAR DEALER - FREEDOM TO SPEND

'In our dealership we have a "slush" budget. Any employee can authorize expenditure from it in favour of a customer. Previously, if a customer came in complaining a hub cap was missing there would be countless arguments as to whether the customer was responsible, or the service department, or sales. Now we cut through all that crap and whoever the customer first complains to can authorize the replacement.'

General Manager, BMW Dealership, Maidenhead

CABLE TV - WHO TO DEAL WITH?

'The salesperson came and convinced us to sign up for cable television. He promised installation within two weeks. It took four and a half months. He took our deposit and then seemed to forget about us. Nobody bothered to communicate with us about the reason for the delay and every time I rang and asked for the salesperson, he was out and I was put through to a different person. Eventually, I tried to speak to the Chairman. His P.A. was really effective and ensured we were connected up within two days. But she was the seventh person in the company I had had to speak to.'

PARCEL COMPANY - FOREVER EXPLAINING

'This parcel company tried to deliver a parcel. I was out. They poked a card through my letterbox asking me to ring a telephone number. I did and explained that I was out most days. I asked if they could deliver it before 8.00am. The lady at the other end listened and then put me through to someone else. I had to wait a minute before the phone was answered. I explained again. Apparently I was speaking to the wrong person, so I was put through to someone else. This third person couldn't commit to an early delivery. She would have to put a request in to the delivery people. The parcel eventually came at 8.05am three days later, just as I was about to leave for work.'

'We found this place for lunch. Annexed to the pub was a restaurant. Two out of the twenty tables were taken. We sat down at one of the tables, talked and then studied the menus. For ten minutes no one had served us. We saw a waitress serve another table. She stared at us and walked away. Another waitress was standing at a till. She was staring at us but did nothing.

'My colleague went to speak to her. She came across appearing very disgruntled . . . "I am not supposed to do this," she said, "but I will take your order". She was obviously reluctant to do so. "What's the problem?" I asked.

"You're supposed to order the food at the counter over there, then we'll bring it to you."

(The counter was hidden from sight)

"How are we supposed to know that?" I asked.

'She pulled out a small folded card which was wedged between the salt cellar and pepper pot. The word "Occupied" was written on the card. She inverted the folded card to reveal, inside, in small print, the procedure for ordering meals.

'We ignorant customers were supposed to know all this. Nobody took the initiative to tell us what the ordering procedure was.'

Test 12

Little extras

'Customer expectations should frequently be exceeded by the provision of unsolicited little extras.'

As soon as customers routinely expect those little extras they become an intrinsic part of the basic service.

Companies and their staff should take delight in pleasing their customers. In itself, the basic product or service provided by the company and purchased by the customer might not always be pleasurable. What is pleasurable, however, is when the customer receives something good over and above that expected.

One of the most exciting aspects of customer service, therefore, is to discover innovative little ways of pleasing the customer even more. This can be a real test for any progressive customer caring company. The provision of unsolicited little extras is a creative and challenging opportunity all staff can enthusiastically respond to. It enables people to be themselves, to give of themselves, to express themselves in a way that is pleasing to the customer. It enables staff to put themselves out for the customer.

Life is full of opportunity. It always has been and always will be. Similarly, the area of customer service is full of opportunity. It is the opportunity of outclassing the competition with a service that provides that little extra. It is the opportunity of exceeding customer expectations. It is the opportunity of enabling your staff, little by little to make a really creative contribution to the company's success. It is the opportunity of rewarding your customers who have proved very loyal over the years. It is these little customer service extras that are the big test for any company.

Some personal challenges

- This is the part of the book you should enjoy most. Get your team together and brainstorm out 100 opportunities for doing a little extra for your customers. Short-list the five opportunities that you are going to do something about in the next four weeks.
- Repeat the process in a month's time, reviewing progress and identifying all the little extras you have done for your customers (whether on the original list or not).

NB Don't ever believe that the reservoir of opportunities will be exhausted. There's always more to come.

REMEMBER:
Little extras cost very little but yield great dividends.

100 LITTLE THINGS YOU CAN DO TO IMPROVE SERVICE

1. **Call customers by their name;**
2. **Ensure staff always give their name when dealing with a customer;**
3. **Wear name badges;**
4. **Serve coffee/tea in reception;**
5. **Assign someone in the front-line to be a 'queue buster';**
6. **Obtain names and addresses of regular customers and send them Christmas cards;**
7. **Send regular customers the occasional present;**
8. **Phone up customers after a large purchase and enquire how they're getting along with it (a car, a video, a computer, a central heating system etc.);**
9. **Just get around and talk to your customers;**
10. **Ring your customers regularly, see how they're getting along;**
11. **Take an interest in your customers when completing a transaction (talk about holidays, children, the weather, the purchase and what it's going to be used for);**

12 Smile;
13 Welcome them properly to the showroom, store, office-building;
14 Listen to your customers;
15 Write to them occasionally - using personal letters;
16 Provide small vacuum cleaners for service engineers;
17 Supply drinks for queueing customers;
18 Deposit bowls of sweets (or fruit) here and there;
19 Put vases of flowers here and there;
20 Make comments cards easily available;
21 Arrange for play equipment for children in waiting areas;
22 Improve signage;
23 Send personalized greetings cards to existing customers;
24 Invite customers to special events;
25 Create 'special' offers for local customers;
26 Get the boss to spend one day a month on the front line;
27 Implement no smoking areas;
28 Check the toilets more frequently;
29 Get more up-to-date magazines in reception;
30 Improve access for people in wheelchairs;
31 Improve facilities for the blind ('braille' signs on railings, in lifts etc.);
32 Pick up litter when you see it;
33 Be the first to get a customer problem fixed;
34 Undertake regular customer service reviews with your team;
35 Check out your own customer service anonymously;
36 Encourage your people to chat to customers;
37 Make company customer documentation more friendly and easier to use;
38 Test customer facilities more frequently;
39 Produce more creative giveaways;
40 Develop a system of identifying regular customers;
41 Don't let the customer do it, do it for them (find it for them on the shelves);
42 Open the door for customers;
43 Always say 'Hello' or 'Good morning' etc.;
44 Chat to their kids;
45 Just be friendlier;
46 Open the doors before time (don't have your security guards jangling keys and staring at the queuing customers one minute before opening);

47 **Send customers a small free sample of one of your products;**
48 **Provide doodling pads and pencils;**
49 **Reply to completed customer questionnaires;**
50 **Fix a customer's problem, even if not directly connected with your business (for example, if a customer's car breaks down on your premises - help them out);**
51 **Champion the customer's cause with your boss;**
52 **End all telephone shunts;**
53 **Acknowledge all customer letters within 24 hours;**
54 **Ring up when you're going to be late;**
55 **Leave the place cleaner than before you started the work for the customer;**
56 **Gift wrap purchases;**
57 **Free toys for adults;**
58 **Free toys for children;**
59 **Unsolicited gifts after the purchase (as a thank-you);**
60 **Free car parking spaces (when non-customers have to pay);**
61 **Offer herbal teas;**
62 **Have mineral water always available;**
63 **Carry the customer's bags to the car;**
64 **All tips to be refused;**
65 **Offer your customer a seat;**
66 **Have a sign in reception welcoming visitors by name;**
67 **Have your Chief Executive write to thank customers for their cooperation;**
68 **Take your manager to meet your customers;**
69 **Drop by when unexpected to find how the customers are getting along with your product/service;**
70 **Organize a family summer event for your regular customers;**
71 **Have a 'customers' comments' book on the front reception;**
72 **Show the customers behind the scenes;**
73 **Introduce customers to the team working behind the scenes;**
74 **Send customers pens, pencils or notebooks with their name on them, as well as yours;**
75 **Get some positive publicity for your customers;**
76 **Provide courtesy transport;**
77 **Automatically confirm meetings in writing with a map of how to get to your office on the back of the letter;**
78 **Send thank-you letters after every meeting;**
79 **Sit in your bath and think about your customers;**
80 **Set yourself a simple customer test every week;**

81 Send your regular customers a discount voucher;
82 On receiving complaints immediately ring customers or go and see them;
83 Always tell the truth;
84 Get your customers to nominate employees of the month;
85 Invite customers to service awards ceremonies for employees;
86 Improve facilities for parents with screaming kids;
87 Put a video in reception;
88 Set up cubicles for confidential conversations (rather than conduct them across the counter);
89 Always keep a note of what customers say and take action as promised;
90 Help out your colleagues in dealing with customers;
91 Provide live music for customers (e.g. a harpist in reception);
92 Serve a customer yourself;
93 Get your customers involved in improving the service;
94 Take your customers out one evening;
95 Always turn up a little early;
96 Develop sensitive antennae towards your customers;
97 Take one new customer initiative every day;
98 Send regular newsletters to customers;
99 Display on the walls photographs of happy customers;
100 Send your customers a copy of this book.

Test 13

Attention to detail

'The fine detail of customer service should always be near to perfect.'

Pareto's Law applies here. 80 per cent of customer alienation comes from getting 20 per cent of the detail wrong.

- The hotel does not have a non-smoking room available as you requested.
- Once again they spell your name incorrectly.
- They send the wrong type of toner for your copying machine.
- The service engineer leaves greasy finger marks all over your equipment.
- Your fork in the restaurant is dirty, the lip of the glass they serve your drink in is chipped.
- There is a light bulb missing in the bedside lamp in your hotel room.
- The airline has no record that you requested an aisle seat when making the reservation. No aisle seats are available.
- You find the ten-pack of oranges in the supermarket does not have a price-code tag, having queued ten minutes to pay for your groceries.
- When you get home you find that two of the oranges in the ten-pack are going bad.
- The railway timetable is incorrect, there is no 17.46 service.

- The new microwave has a scratch down the side.
- They forget to order the replacement hub-cap for your car and then eventually obtain the wrong one.
- One of the headlamp washers is missing on your new car.
- They charge you full English breakfast when you only had Continental.
- The wake-up call does not come.
- The pen on the chain in the bank has dried up.
- After making a special journey to collect an application form, you find they have run out of them.
- You are a stranger in town. The bus-driver does not shout out your stop, as requested.
- The book you bought by mail-order is defective, the first few pages being stuck together.
- They get your name wrong.
- They lose your file.

Along with those little extras, it is attention to detail that distinguishes a really superb customer service organization from a poor one.

By getting the detail right you ensure that you get everything else right. Failure to get the detail right can be due to a number of factors:

- A failure to listen attentively to customers and make detailed notes of their requirements – especially if they vary from the standard.
- A failure to communicate effectively with the providers of service (salesperson to distribution, travel agent to airline, telephonist to service department, waiter to chef).

- A failure to establish detailed standards and check that they are being adhered to (the hotel room TV is working, the cleanliness of the cutlery, tidying up after the repair).
- A failure to realize, overall, that detail is critically important.
- A belief that striving for perfection is too costly.

In too many cases it is the detail that induces the customer to make a judgement about the standard of the organization's services. He or she will take the basic standards of service for granted and it is the deviations from these standards, albeit often minor, that will make the customer aware that the service is better or worse than expected.

Small aberrations of service, while not intrinsically important in terms of the finished product of service can be incredibly irritating and cause customers to form exaggerated opinions of the organization.

Some managers are frightened of addressing the details of customer service for fear of appearing petty-minded and fault-finding. They fear alienating their staff if, as managers, they go round pointing out detailed faults. In their view, no-one is perfect and there has to be a degree of toleration in how you manage sometimes imperfect staff.

The skill is in developing an awareness among your team as to how important it is to get the detail right, and therefore how important it is to receive feedback on the extent to which this is being achieved.

Management is not only about 'what' you say and do, but also 'how' you say and do it. When it comes to addressing issues of detail, it is important not to appear pernickety and do it in a way that does not alienate.

Some personal challenges

- Discuss with your team the importance of getting the detail right as far as the customer is concerned. Brainstorm out on a flip-chart as many of the details that you can think of.
- Working with your team, establish a set of detailed standards for every aspect of customer service you are responsible for providing (internally or externally). You do not need to establish these as a formal written policy, but perhaps just keep a note of them for future reference at team discussions.
- Working with your team, undertake an immediate check to find out whether these standards are currently being adhered to throughout your area of responsibility. Be meticulous about this.
- Review the findings with your team and decide upon further action.

REMEMBER:
Attention to detail is the ultimate test of a really caring attitude towards the customer.

THE STORIES CUSTOMERS TELL . . .

INVOICE PROBLEM - THE DETAIL

'We notified all our clients of our change of address. Six months later we sent an invoice to one of our clients. The invoice clearly stated our new address. After six weeks we had not been paid. We chased it up and discovered that the cheque had been sent to our old address. Apparently, as soon as our company name had been put into the computer it had registered us as an existing supplier - and this was listed with our old address. Apparently, the person we sent our change of address to had not notified finance, and the invoice clerk in finance had not bothered to compare the address in the computer with that on the invoice.'

HOTEL - SMALL THINGS MISSING

'For the second time running I checked into my room at this hotel to find there were no soaps or shampoos in the bathroom. Later, when I ordered tea in the coffee shop, they failed to bring me any milk. Finally on Sunday morning there was no colour supplement with my paper.'

CAR SERVICE - MISSING VALVE CAPS

'I collected my car from service and when I got home I found that two of the valve caps on the tyres had not been put on. It meant another journey back to the garage.'

NO CHEQUE ATTACHED

'They wrote me a letter agreeing to a refund and saying a cheque was attached. It wasn't.'

FAX MACHINE - MISSING COMPONENTS

'They delivered the new fax/copier to our office. The engineer arrived an hour after the delivery team had gone. He went to connect up the machine only to find that in the components box there was no power cable nor telephone connector. His journey was wasted. It took another two days before the machine was properly installed.'

Test 14

Immaculate appearance

'The appearance of everything the customer sees in the company should be immaculate.'

When things don't look good, customers often make the assumption that they aren't good. When people don't look good, customers often make the assumption that they are no good at providing the service required.

Appearance is vital in securing a customer's confidence that the service to be provided is reliable and of high quality. When the carpets begin to fray, the uniforms are scruffy, the paint is peeling, the company transport unwashed and the letterhead 'cheap and nasty', customers will begin to have doubts about the company's capability of providing an effective service.

Appearance relates to every aspect of the company's business. Heaps of paper and files scattered across an untidy office will leave an impression which the customer will relate to service, overflowing waste bins will also tell the customer something. Employees with long scruffy hair and dirty shoes will create an impression of low standards and disinterest in high quality.

Really successful companies strive to achieve an immaculate appearance in every facet of their business, developing and maintaining clean and pleasant reception facilities, attractive buildings and ensuring that their employees have smart uniforms to wear.

The appearance is reflected in high standard company documentation and all aspects of the company's approach to marketing.

Some personal challenges

- How do you think you, your team and your company appear to your customers?
- Do you really go out of your way to maintain the highest standards of appearance?
- Take one step today to improve appearance in the eyes of your customers.

REMEMBER:
Customers will often judge the service by the appearance of the company.

THE STORIES CUSTOMERS TELL . . .

DIRTY BUSES

'When I see their dirty buses puffing black clouds of smoke into the town, the last thing I am tempted to do is travel on them.'

BADLY DRESSED CONDUCTOR

'The conductor checking our tickets hardly inspired me with confidence. He was unshaven, had a self-rolled fag in his mouth, even though it was a non-smoking area. He had no jacket on and was sweating at the armpits. For footwear he wore delapidated training shoes and white socks with holes in. The only semblance of uniform was his unpressed and heavily stained navy trousers which were much too short for him. I just wondered what he would do if there was an emergency.'

HOTEL - DIRTY ALL OVER

'We went to this hotel on the South Coast. I had an inkling it wouldn't be good when I saw the litter in the car park. The service in the restaurant was abominably slow and, most embarrassingly, when I went to the toilet there was no paper in any of the cubicles. The floors of the toilets were wet and the washbasins stained with greasemarks. I don't think anyone had cleaned the toilet for days. Somehow, when things go wrong like this you start looking for other things wrong. The tables in the coffee shop had not been cleared of dirty plates, there were crumbs and fragments of food all over the floor. The pathways between the hotel and the residential accommodation was full of weeds. In the end I complained. The manager just listened politely to me but did nothing about it.'

Part 2

MANAGING TO ACHIEVE INCREDIBLE CUSTOMER SERVICE

'Achieving incredibly good customer service is a direct result of having incredibly good managers.'

The interrelationship between customer service and management is so vital that organizations ignore it at their peril. Too many companies have attempted to improve customer service without addressing fundamental issues requiring management change.

Exhorting front-line staff to smile more, while continuing with traditionally bad management practices, will achieve the opposite of that intended.

In Part Two we deal with the essential of *MANAGING to achieve incredible customer service*.

15

The undying obsession

'The only way to succeed with customers is to provide continually "service to the point of obsession".'

One run around the block will never make you fit. A daily run over a period of time will.

During the 1980s, many companies took just one run at improving customer service. They mounted expensive campaigns for a few months and exhorted their front-line staff to smile more, to be friendlier and to provide better information. Glossy videos and wall-posters proclaiming the importance of the customer became the order of the day.

A year later such initiatives were forgotten. Other campaigns (such as cost-cutting) had taken over.

Any study of success in the field of customer service (for example, BMW, British Airways, British Gas) will demonstrate that customer service is something that has to be continually addressed – over years if not decades. British Gas has been pushing customer service for almost 20 years – and to good effect. BMW has also developed a reputation for providing exceptionally good customer service over a long period of time.

To really succeed, the pursuit of excellence in customer service must really become an undying obsession. It requires every single person in the organization to focus their energies and their enthusiasm on not just getting it right, but improving it. Customer service consequently becomes a dominating theme throughout the organization; continually debated, continually reviewed, continually challenged – and its successes continually celebrated.

Such obsession means that no single opportunity should be passed without underlining a key point on customer service. When a letter of compliment comes in it should be widely acclaimed internally. Staff should be encouraged to be friendly to customers, to treat customers like friends rather than enemies. Staff should be supported in taking initiatives on behalf of their customers, rather than constrained (by having to seek permission) in doing so.

The obsession should show through in the company's newsletters, annual reports, training programmes, performance appraisals, sales conferences, staff meetings. In fact, it should permeate every facet of the organization.

The executive who goes through a working day without thinking about customer service, without devoting at least a little time to it, is an executive without obsession.

The obsession means having customer service at the forefront of your mind, today, tomorrow, next month, next year and in ten years time.

Customer service is something you cannot forget, it is not something you can get right today and assume will be right tomorrow. There are always new opportunities, new challenges.

Some personal challenges

- Do you have any obsessions at work?
- Where does customer service rank on this list?
- How are you personally handling your obsession?
- How do you get staff to share your obsession for superb customer service?

REMEMBER:
The obsession is a persistent preoccupation with customer service.

WEEKLY DISCUSSIONS ON CUSTOMER SERVICE

'Once a week we get all the staff together to discuss service to our customers. Customer Service is so obviously important that there is danger you forget about it, take for granted it's happening, become complacent.

At our weekly meetings we are continually relearning what we know already. That's how obsessive we are about customer service.'

General Manager, BMW Dealership, Maidenhead

16

Overriding commitment at the top

'There is no escape from this. Unless there is an overriding commitment to customer service at the top of the organization the actual service provided will at best be mediocre.'

The obsession with customer service should show through with an overriding commitment at the top of the organization. The 'top' is not only the Chief Executive, but the 20–30 most senior executives in the organization. By achieving such a critical mass of commitment at the top, the probability is that the rest of the organization will become committed.

If the 'top' contains people who are less committed than the Chief Executive, there is a danger that conflicting signals will be sent through the organization and decisions will be made at the expense of serving the customer.

Top-level commitment to customer service must therefore be real. It must be visible and it must be tangible. The commitment of the top team must be evident in the way they set their budgets and targets. It must be evident in the way they talk and in the communications they emit. It is critical that it is evident in the decisions they make and the actions they take.

They must avoid like the plague any accusation or perception of lip-service commitment. The risk of this is high in times of recession when budgets are cut back and customer service activities can be viewed as an expensive luxury.

The top team's commitment should therefore come from the depths of their hearts as well as the remotest corners of their minds.

Top executives should be seen out and about, demonstrating their commitment to customers and to the staff serving them. They should set an example by frequently talking and listening to customers and employees. They should be seen supporting customer initiatives throughout the organization. They should be seen praising customer service achievements and recognizing the contribution of those that improve service.

Top executives need to express their commitment to customer service with clearly articulated visions and strategies for it, together with well-developed corporate standards which are striven for throughout the organization and monitored frequently.

To reinforce their commitment to customer service they should be prepared to learn about it and prepared to accept the potentially unpalatable truths about organization shortfalls.

Ideally, that commitment should be exhibited with immense passion and enthusiasm, such that it invigorates and energizes the whole organization.

Foremost, top executives must reveal their commitment to customer service by the high proportion of time they devote to it. In that sense, the commitment becomes overriding.

It should also override those negative penny-conscious accountants who equate success to cost constraint, who take delight in trimming indirect costs (fat) and turning organizations into skinny, anorexic, debilitated bureaucracies.

Customer service is an incredibly positive facet of the business and should therefore override any negative attempt to constrain decisions and actions taken in favour of the customer. Investing a little extra in the customer will always pay greater dividends than trying to save costs by cutting back on the service provided.

Some personal challenges

- Be honest. Are you deeply committed to customer service?
- If yes, how do you demonstrate that commitment?
- Does your commitment to provide excellent customer service override other priorities?
- How much time and emotional energy do you really put into achieving incredibly good customer service? Count the hours. If there are few or none, then your organization has a big customer service problem.

REMEMBER:

It's your own personal overriding commitment to customer service that will make all the difference in achieving incredibly good customer service for your organization.

17

A strategic vision

'Incredible customer service can only be achieved with a clear vision of what it means to your organization in the long term and a clear strategy to achieve this.'

For any organization, customer service requires a clear definition: a present definition and a future definition.

That future definition is a customer service vision clarifying what you want to achieve over the next few years.

The present definition is an in-depth analysis and assessment of your service levels today.

Inevitably, a strategy is required to move from the present to the future.

It is imperative that the vision is clear, has meaning and is substantially more than a mere slogan to be embroidered on wallpaper. The vision should provide a focus on what you want to attain, over the coming years, in delivering the best service to your customers.

Effectively, it represents an ideal of how you want your customers and your people to see your organization in a few years time.

As an ideal, it is a moving horizon, something you move towards but never quite attain in your continual quest for improvement.

One important criteria of the vision is that it is something you (and your people) personally want to achieve, which is of vital importance to your customers. Furthermore, it should be something you are confident you personally can make substantial progress towards achieving.

While a vision should be an 'ideal' for the future, it should not be treated as a fantasy (a dream unlikely to be realized – like winning the pools). The key thing about a vision is that you can make substantial progress towards achieving it. It is an 'ideal' in the sense that there is always more to be achieved. The more you achieve, the more you discover there is to achieve. You can be the best today (having achieved your vision of the 'gold medal') and fall flat on your face tomorrow.

The vision should be ongoing and capable of evolutionary development.

An example of a service vision is given in Figure 17.1.

Having identified and confirmed the service vision a management strategy should be developed for moving towards this vision.

As the vision will essentially be long-term, not all the service goals within it necessarily have to be achieved short-term. The achievement of the visionary goals should therefore be prioritized, based on criteria relating to maximum positive impact on the customer. This prioritization should produce one or two short-term visionary goals for achievement within a year (see Figure 17.2). These will need to be costed out and budgeted for. A clear management plan of action for achieving these initial goals, as well as the longer term ones will need to be developed and communicated. Such a plan should include the development of the appropriate information systems, training programmes, customer feedback processes and performance measures for monitoring progress.

There are a number of ways of developing a customer service vision. Perhaps the most widely used is for the top team to go away for a couple of days to thrash out a draft vision. Further two day sessions are then run at which senior executives present the draft vision to groups of managers and invite them to consider it and make suggestions for developing it into a final version. The role of each group of managers would be to 'test' the draft vision in relation to their own jobs and assess the feasibility of pursuing it departmentally.

One of the key tests for a vision is that it can be articulated in a simple way and have practical meaning for every person in the organization. In other words, every employee should be able to read the vision and say 'This applies to me and my job.'

Once the vision has been firmed up, it should be communicated throughout the organization and a series of workshops or training sessions scheduled to provide an opportunity for every employee to discuss it and consider the application of it to their jobs. Such a process engenders a positive attitude towards the achievement of the customer service vision and thereby attains the necessary commitment.

Some personal challenges

- Sit down with your own team and thrash out an outline service vision for your current area of responsibility (no matter how small or large).
- To ensure the vision is both meaningful and credible test out the service vision on:
  - your own boss;
  - front-line people in your department.
- Having firmed up on the vision by taking into account the views of your boss and your people, develop a clear management strategy for achieving it.
- Review the vision every six months and develop it further, constantly striving to push up the standards and establishing more demanding visionary goals.

REMEMBER:
If you don't have a vision you don't know where you are going.

THE VISION

Provide an exceptionally responsive service to our customers.

By this we mean:

(a) Always arriving on time
(b) Courtesy at all times
(c) The highest quality of work
(d) Putting ourselves out for the customer
(e) Prices that are perceived by the customer as fair
(f) High standards of appearance by all our staff
(g) Demonstrating a sensitive and responsive attitude towards our customers

COMPANY GOALS

A PUNCTUALITY

Improve monitoring procedure for arrival time at customers.
On-time arrivals to improve from 73% to 90% within 12 months.

B COURTESY

All staff to participate in half-day 'Customer Relations' workshops within 12 months.

C HIGHEST QUALITY OF WORK

5% of calls to be subjected to 'Quality Inspection' follow-up visit to customer by supervisor.
Number of repeat calls (reoccurrence of problem) to be reduced from 9% to 5% in 12 months.
All engineers to be given one-day training course in 'Quality Servicing'.
Achieve BS5750 within 12 months.

D PUTTING OURSELVES OUT FOR THE CUSTOMER

Survey our customers: 'Is there more we could do?' Survey report within 12 months.
Solicit views from all staff and summarize their views in survey report.

E VALUE FOR MONEY

Improve method for obtaining 'intelligence' data on competitors' prices.
Survey customers on their perceptions about our prices.

F **APPEARANCE**

Line managers to consult staff on ways of improving appearance.
No smoking policy to be introduced.
Establish standard that all company vehicles washed at least once a week.
No company vehicle with any defect (no matter how minor) to be allowed out on road.

G **RESPONSIVENESS**

Improve telephone response times to 5 seconds.
Improve documentation response times to 2 days.

FINANCE AND SYSTEMS

Improve invoicing procedures to be more explicit on charging.
Review switchboard procedures and recommend improvements to board to achieve 5 second standard.

PERSONNEL

Develop test in all selection procedures to ensure potential recruits are 'customer-oriented'.
Set up Customer Relation workshops and Quality Service Training.
Introduce no smoking policy.

SALES

Review competitors' pricing and report to Board.

CONTROL ROOM

Review call-out procedures and implement opportunities for improvement to achieve punctuality standards.

CUSTOMER SERVICE DEPARTMENT

Conduct surveys and report to Board.
Review current standards of customer documentation and initiate improvements to achieve 2 days standard.
Coordinate all customer service initiatives and report to Board.

OPERATIONS MANAGERS

Regular team meetings on customer service with focus on courtesy, responsiveness, appearance and quality.
Initiate 1 in 20 'Quality Inspection' visits by supervisors.

Figure 17.1 Service engineering company

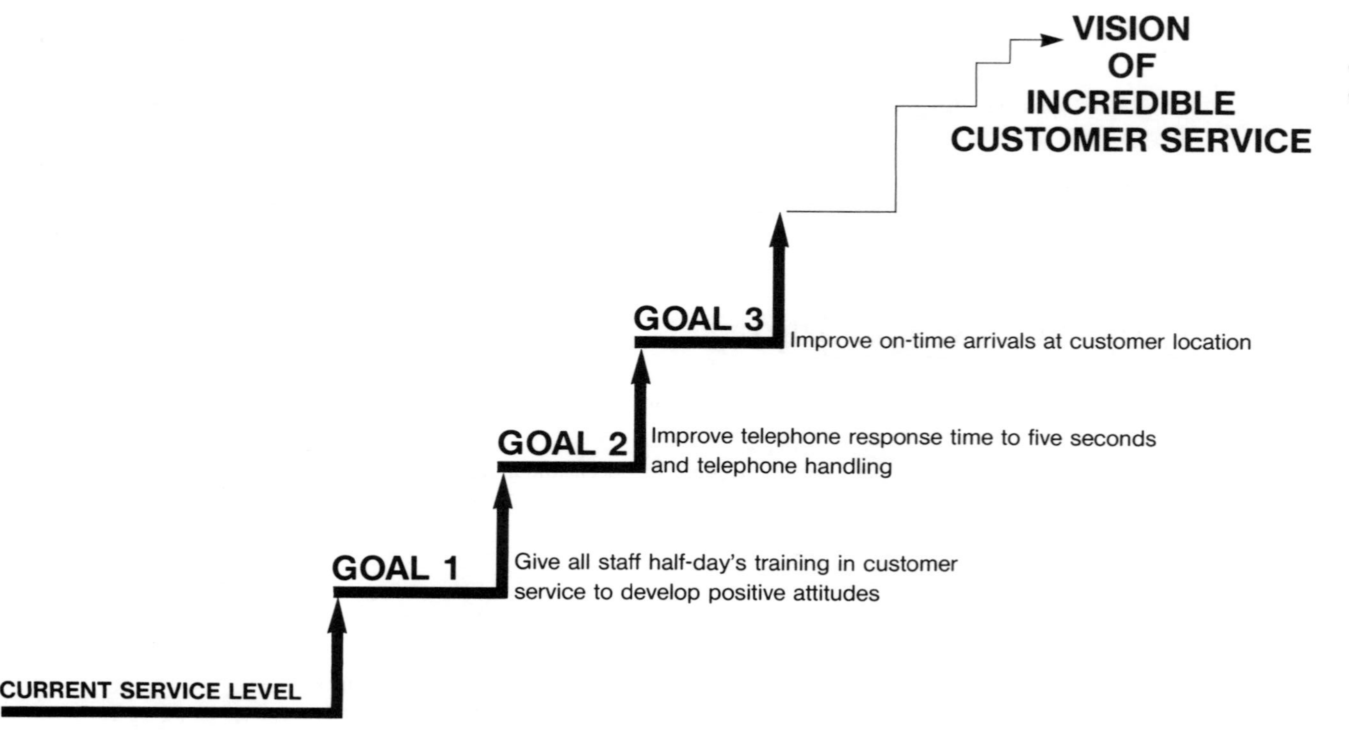

Figure 17.2 Priority goals

18

Clear corporate goals

***'Clearly defined and measurable goals must be set to achieve* incredible customer service.'**

Incredible customer service is neither a fantasy nor a wish. Nor is it an exhortation or a buzz-phrase to be imprinted on badges, T-shirts and wall certificates.

Incredible customer service is the achievement of specific goals within the customer service vision and therefore can only be achieved if these goals are clearly and unambiguously set. The first part of this book specifies 14 critical goals which, in the author's view, are immutable, in other words applicable to every organization.

In addition to these key goals, there will be company specific goals – targets which are unique to the company or industry, which characterize the service and add value to the transactions undertaken with customers.

Company specific goals will vary from one customer group to another. Thus for a hotel, the service available in higher tariff 'executive rooms' will be by definition of a higher level than that provided to standard rooms. The same applies to a service engineering company which might offer a 'five-star premium maintenance' contract or a basic 'job and time' call-out service. Elsewhere, for example, distribution companies might trade on a high-tariff, 'same day' delivery service, while others might trade on a lower tariff, four day service.

Company specific service goals should also differentiate between:

- Pre-sales service standards (for example, showroom comfort, coffee availability, quality of information provided etc.)
- Sales service standards (such as speed of processing orders, quality of sales documentation, level of guarantee, actual delivery times, user-friendliness of manuals etc.)
- After-sales service standards (for example customer help lines, sales follow-up calls, ease of callout etc.)

Additionally they should differentiate between:

- Standards for reactive responses (effectiveness in responding to customer-initiated demands for service).
- Standards for proactive initiatives (effectiveness in providing unsolicited company-initiated services for the customer).

Considerations of cost are critical in developing company specific service goals, whereas attainment of the fourteen basic standards should be attempted at all cost. Expressed another way, a customer should expect to pay more for an added value 'first-class' service, but not more for the basics of customer service. A five second telephone response would be considered such a basic and should be provided irrespective of the class of service being offered.

In developing a strategic vision of service, therefore, a company must decide upon its overall service philosophy, for example whether to move towards a high quality service, selling at a premium, or switching to a lower cost more basic standard of service, or offering the customer a choice of both.

Within the organization, there should also be goals specific to departments, including internal services between departments. For example:

- Delivery times for internal mail;
- Queueing times in staff restaurant;

- Lead times on making internal appointments;
- Target dates for the provision of regular financial data;
- Lead times for getting documents typed in the typing pool;
- Response times for getting repairs to buildings.

It must be emphasized that whatever the vision, achieving the goals represented by the fourteen key tests of customer service must be a priority.

Whilst managers would accept the importance of goal-setting (or target setting, or standard setting) the danger is that too many goals are set, thereby causing dissipation of effort and potential confusion of purpose.

In the absence of any clearly defined corporate or department customer service goals, it would be unwise to suddenly proclaim the fourteen basic goals as corporate targets. Few, if any, would be achieved.

The long-term service vision should be carefully reviewed and, within it, short-term priority goals established, with perhaps only one or two critical goals being set in the first place, (such as 'Our initial priority goal is to get our telephones sorted out and improve response times as well as telephone handling'). See Figure 17.2.

This immediate goal (which will be the first step en route to achieving a vision of incredible customer service) is one which:

- will have the most beneficial impact on the bottom line;
- will be most appreciated by the customer;
- all staff can relate to and want themselves to achieve;
- achieve credibility for senior managers in demonstrating that they are prepared to 'put their money where their mouth is'.

Too often, senior managers proclaim their intentions about customer service and then appear to do little about it.

By specifying one or two critical goals to begin with, managers can galvanize the organization, concentrating everyone's mind on a critical aspect of customer service.

As soon as substantial progress has been made towards achieving these few goals, then additional goals can be set.

Setting the corporate goals one by one enables:

- A highly focused approach
- A simple approach everyone can understand (no confusion, no conflicting priorities).

Having declared the first clear corporate customer service goals, it is imperative that senior managers:

- Communicate and involve everyone in achieving these goals.
- Invest in the achievement of these goals (training, systems etc.).
- Provide feedback on progress made in achieving them.

Figure 18.1 on page 80 provides some definitions and examples of what is meant by vision, goals, standards and culture.

Some personal challenges

- Are you aware of what currently is the most important customer service goal in your organization? (If you are unaware, then the company is not really concerned about customer service).
- What are the most important customer service goals you currently have in your department? (Again, if you do not have such goals you cannot claim to be driven by customer service).

- How often do you receive feedback about progress made in attaining these goals? (If you receive no feedback, make an effort to obtain it).

REMEMBER:
Tomorrow, if not today, you can score a goal for a customer!

	DEFINITIONS	EXAMPLES
STRATEGIC VISION (Long-term) 12 months +	Long term strategic aim Mission Sense of direction Moving horizon OVERALL STRATEGIC PURPOSE	To achieve an incredibly high standard of service to the company's customers with specific reference to: • Product quality in general • Reliability • Responsiveness to all customer needs • Positive attitude at all times • Constant innovation
GOALS (Short-term) Up to 12 months	Short-term aim Short-term objective Target Something very specific to be achieved MEASURABLE SHORT-TERM ATTAINMENT	• Making packaging easier to remove • Reduce returns from 3% to 1% • Establish customer service desks at each branch • Half-day 'customer care' workshops for all staff
STANDARDS (Ongoing)	Quality measure Something to be achieved day-by-day MEASURABLE ONGOING LEVEL OF ATTAINMENT	• No shortages on delivery • 99.5% products ex-factory defect free • All telephones answered within 5 seconds • 90% customers surveyed report positive attitudes shown by company employees
CULTURE (Evolutionary)	Existing values amongst various groups/individuals Existing beliefs held by various groups/individuals What is considered important by various groups/individuals within organization Actual (rather than prescribed) basis for existing practices Attitudes throughout organization Organization norms Organization ethos THE UNDERLYING THINKING IN THE ORGANIZATION	• Team-briefing meetings are too often cancelled • We rarely see our boss • The company is only interested in short-term profit • It's not hard work that's important here but the impression you make on your bosses at meetings • They pay lip-service to customer service • There's nothing we can do to make improvements, they will only stop us.

Figure 18.1 Definitions and examples

19

Creating a customer service culture

'The value of incredible customer service should be deeply embedded within the culture of the organization and within the personal beliefs of every serving member of that organization.'

An organization culture cannot be prescribed or imposed. It evolves as a reflection of the values and beliefs directly and indirectly exhibited by senior executives, as well as in the reactions of the rest of the organization to these values and beliefs.

Words are limited in evolving a culture. Behaviour, actions and decisions as a reflection of beliefs and values are much more significant. Conflicting behaviour at senior level (saying one thing, doing another) leads to a culture of cynicism, distrust and corporate inaction.

At senior level, consistent behaviour which reflects the beliefs and values held by people lower in the organization will, without too much direction, induce and reinforce similar patterns of behaviour at these lower levels.

Senior executives therefore have a critical impact on the culture (behaviours, beliefs, values) of the organization. A few loose conflicting words, one or two contradictory decisions can produce a pathological reaction which begins to destroy the desired culture.

Too many senior executives are ignorant of the impact their behaviour, words, actions and decisions have upon the vital culture of their organization.

Customer service provides an excellent 'seeding' opportunity for developing a strong positive culture for ongoing success.

To create such a culture, senior executives, their managers and their teams need to 'think, talk and breathe' customer service continually, such that the lifeblood of the organization (its words, decisions, actions and the behaviours of its people) keeps the concept of customer service alive.

With such a culture, customer service becomes a focus for developing the company's customer base and market, it becomes a focus for performance management, as well as training and communications, it becomes a focus for the everyday attention of most people in the organization – from Chief Executive to frontline. As a result, no decision is taken without exploring the impact of that decision on the customer and the service provided.

Edicts, policies, memos, notices, manuals, training courses, conferences, recruitment, rewards, strategies, investments, manufacturing, product development, sales, distribution – in fact, virtually every facet of the organization's function, becomes geared towards the customer when such a culture exists.

The whole organization begins to 'live' customer service. Employees and managers are continually aware of it. Whichever way you turn in a customer-oriented organization, you will discover some crucial aspect of customer service. You will find it in manufacturing, in their attention to reliability and quality. You will find it in warehousing and distribution, in their attention to delivery times and ease of ordering. You will find it in research, in their attention to product design and ease of use. You will find it in service engineering, in their attention to the effectiveness of repairs and their responsiveness to customers. You will find it in the way the finance department handles invoices and collects debts. You will find it in personnel, in the way they recruit and the way they establish training. You will inevitably find it in all your encounters at reception, on the telephone and in corresponding with the company. You will even see it in the eyes of the cleaner who looks up, smiles, offers a few words of greeting and directs you to the appropriate office when you have lost your way.

Some personal challenges

- Most importantly, you will find the customer service culture reflected in yourself and everything you do.
- That is your personal challenge. You have to realize that your attitude and behaviour alone, in the organization, can create, reinforce or destroy a customer service culture.

REMEMBER:
You are part of the customer service culture.

20

Prescriptions and freedoms

'Incredible customer service is not something that can be prescribed from the top but is more the product of a wide range of freedoms exercised by front-line people.'

Major bureaucracies essentially constrain their people. Decision-making tends to gravitate up towards the centre of the organization through a labyrinth of procedures and rules which stifle people from exercising any freedoms to please the customer. The customer always suffers; it takes a long time to get decisions made, let alone get anything done. Anything that falls outside the 'system' creates a problem, and frequently customers create demands which do not fit into the system (such as out of hours opening).

The prescriptive bureaucratic organization, therefore, can never achieve *incredible customer service*. There is no way senior executives can sit in their elevated towers and prescribe totally the types of customer service decisions front-line people should be making many miles away.

Successful management today is all about creating environments and cultures whereby the people on the front-line have the capabilities and freedoms to meet the specific demands of customers and take initiatives on their behalf.

The key component in such a management approach is trust. Accountability cannot be devolved down through the organization unless those at the 'lower' reaches can be trusted to exercise their newly found freedoms with a degree of skill, as well as with the utmost responsibility. Furthermore, if the tradition in the organization is deferential, subservient, hostile, punitive and autocratic, most front-line people will be reluctant to take on newly assigned freedoms, for fear of making mistakes and being punished. Why take an initiative on behalf of a customer if it gets you into trouble? What is the point of authorizing a very small discount to a customer making a large purchase if your manager then reprimands you? What is the point of authorizing an up-grade for a severely dissatisfied customer if you then get told off for it?

Too many organizations, even today, allow their people no latitude in pleasing the customers. Their people have to follow the rules and that's that.

While total freedom without control would undoubtedly produce anarchy, the essential task for any manager seeking to improve customer service is to create a culture whereby decision-making accountability can be moved towards the right of the following spectrum, therefore creating more freedoms at the front-line to satisfy customers.

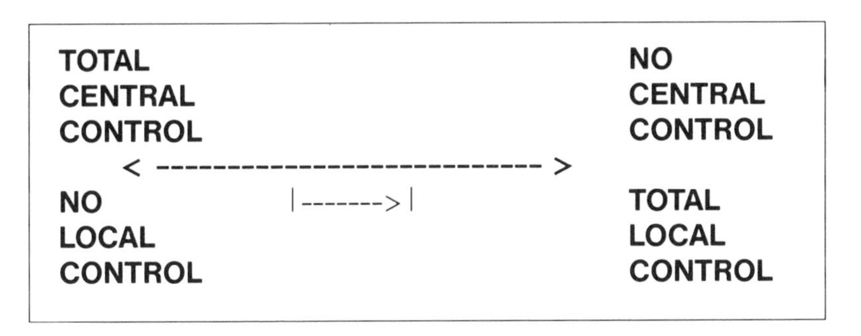

Figure 20.1 Control spectrum

There are a whole series of freedoms which potentially can be devolved down through the organization in order to improve customer satisfaction. These can relate to:

FREEDOM AREAS

PEOPLE	**Hiring** **Rewarding** **Training** **etc.**
MONEY	**Budget accountability** **Moving funds within and between budget headings** **Refunds** **Discounts** **Expenditure** **etc.**
COMMUNICATIONS	**Leaflets** **Letters to customers** **Employee workshops** **Customer surveys** **etc.**
PROPERTY	**Refurbishment** **Repairs** **Office allocation** **Layout** **etc.**
CONSUMABLES	**Choice of** **Acquisition of** **Disposal of**

However, in devolving accountability, it is critical that the organization's information systems are developed to ensure an adequate supply of meaningful data to the front-line. There is no point, for example, in assigning budget accountabilities to front-line supervisors (so that they use some discretion in satisfying their customers), if they are not aware of what their budgets are and where they stand on expenditure in relation to their budgets.

Some personal challenges

- Produce a checklist of the types of decisions that need to be made in your area of responsibility to achieve incredible service.
- Identify which decisions can be devolved further down the line.
- Ensure that your information systems are adequate for supplying meaningful data to the people you are devolving to.

To help you, here are some examples of questions you ought to be asking:

QUESTIONS OF FREEDOM (TO IMPROVE CUSTOMER SERVICE)

WITHOUT SEEKING PERMISSION FROM ABOVE CAN I . . .

1. **USE a cheque book to write a customer a refund?**
2. **SPEND £100 on a team celebration when we've achieved some great customer service?**
3. **SPEND £1000 sending a team member to a professional conference?**
4. **SPEND £800 getting a customer leaflet printed in an ethnic minority language?**
5. **APPROVE an honorarium payment of £500 for some exceptional work?**
6. **AUTHORIZE a small (5%) discount to a customer, or a small privilege, or a small gift?**
7. **USE unspent money in my budget (for example, relating to staff vacancies) for other purposes such as training?**
8. **HIRE temporary staff?**
9. **PURCHASE a new fax machine?**
10. **DELEGATE the types of decisions above to members of my team?**

If you can't do any of the above, it is unlikely that you have the freedom to achieve *incredible customer service*. So your big challenge now is to go out and demonstrate to the powers that be that you can be trusted to make these types of decision to improve customer service.

REMEMBER:

The people who know the customers best should have as much responsibility as possible for pleasing them.

21

Investment in customer service

'Customers are an asset to be invested in.'

It is totally predictable. At every seminar I run, someone in the audience will stick up their hand and say 'You appreciate that the type of improvements you are talking about will cost a lot of money'.

Improvements like speeding up telephone response times, reducing queueing and waiting times, refurbishing reception, developing customer-caring attitudes amongst staff.

Financial people can be a disaster. They see everything in terms of costs. If it is a cost, it must be bad, let's get it down and improve profit. The organization is reduced to a frenzied state of cost-cutting. You get your brownie points for running a lean, mean ship. This means cutting people-related costs, training costs, salaries, benefits and so on. It also means cutting back on the things you do for your customers. 'Surely what the customer wants is the basic product – why should they pay extra for all these frills – and isn't customer service a frill? In the end, does the customer really want to pay for the cost of a glossy five star reception facility? Obsessive cost-cutting can also lead to an anorexic condition where there is no fat in the system to deal with unplanned peaks. There is nothing worse than queueing up for a service with only one out of seven counters open, and nobody available to relieve the hard-pressed person serving at that counter.

You have to make up your own mind what is best for your customers. But before you do so, it would be wise to find out how your customers perceive you, and what their expectations and aspirations are with respect to the service you provide. Ultimately, the issue is how much time, effort and resource you are prepared to invest in giving your customers what they really want and can reasonably expect from a top-rate company. Experience shows that those organizations that invest in customer service reap a high dividend.

This means:

- Investing in training to encourage your staff to think about, contribute to and achieve the highest standards of customer service.
- Investing in developing (and recruiting) top-flight customer-oriented, people-oriented managers and staff you can trust.
- Investing in systems (information, invoicing, monitoring, distribution, telephones, etc.) which ensure that the customer service promise is always kept.
- Investing in little extras (or frills that thrill the customer).
- Investing in an environment which is compatible with the high standards of service which you want the customer to expect of you.
- Investing in a product or service which cannot be rivalled by your competitors and which the customer really values.
- Finally it means investing in an adequate level of resources (with sufficient reserve capability) to undertake the basic operation of the business without delay or detriment to the customer.

As customers acquire an even greater level of disposable income, they are bestowed with an even greater choice of competing products and services. Increasingly, their criterion of choice will be marginal and will rest upon the critical element of customer service.

The customer service differential or gap between yourself and a competitor might be small. It can only be broadened by an investment of company resource – not just of money, but of time. Such an investment will reflect your own passions and commitment to the vital need of improving customer service.

Aspects of investment you might well care to focus on are:

1. Easy access to your product and service:
   (Free-phone numbers, hot-lines, telephone ordering etc.)
2. Quick response to customer needs:
   (Call-out systems, 24 hour deliveries, telephone responses, responses to letters, telephone cover etc.)
3. Customer comfort and convenience factors:
   (Reception, seating, hospitality, decor, transport to and from premises, opening hours, ease of purchase etc.)
4. Company staff:
   (Attitudinal development, communications, training, rewards etc.)
5. Product improvement:
   (Reliability, more features, design, ease of use, manuals etc.)
6. Customer service frills:
   (Gifts, packaging, up-grades etc.)
7. Reparation:
   (Replacement without hesitation, refunds, up-grades etc.)
8. Company systems:
   (Invoicing, customer databases, reservations, telephones, distribution).
9. Communications with customers:
   (Timetables, brochures, mailshots, questionnaires, surveys etc.)
10. Increased resources at the front-line:
    (More people on the counter to reduce queues).

Any board should have a customer service investment strategy as part of its vision. It must be a strategy they believe essential for the long term success of the business. The strategy and the consequential short-term plans for achieving it must be both realizable and recognizable by employees and customers alike. The establishment and implementation of such plans should be widely publicized to achieve credibility for the company's declarations of intent (vision) on customer service.

Some personal challenges

- Find a quiet room and summarize current and future investments on customer service. Categorize these investments as follows:
  - Investments by your company or organization
  - Investments in your department
  - Investments initiated by you.
- What further investments do you need to make to achieve your customer service goals?
- Develop a strategy for persuading the department/company to make further investments (time, money etc.) to help you achieve your goals.

REMEMBER:
Five more minutes of your time today devoted to customer service is an important investment.

PUBLIC SERVICE ORGANIZATION – LACK OF PHOTOCOPIERS

'We have to go down seven floors to get photocopying done here. There are only two machines to service the whole building. Often, one of them is out of action. Almost always there is a long queue, once I had to wait 45 minutes to get some urgent copying done. We have a YTS girl in the department who is supposed to help us get these things done, but often she's at college, or on leave, or preoccupied with other tasks. Then we get no help.

Across the corridor, Personnel have their own photocopier, but they keep it under lock and key and don't let any other department use it. How they got approval when we're all supposed to use the communal photocopiers, I don't know.

No wonder we have complaints that it takes an eternity to get any service out of our legal department.'

(Solicitor in a major public services organization)

22

Feedback on customer service

'Without clear feedback from your customers, service can never be improved.'

It is simply a matter of knowing:

- What your customers want;
- How your customers feel;
- What your customers think;
- How to make your customers feel valued;
- How to listen;
- What sort of initiatives your customers will appreciate.

The more successful customer serving executives open their minds to every conceivable form of feedback, whereas the less successful close theirs off against any feedback which conflicts with their perceptions (it is what the psychologists call cognitive dissonance). These latter types become defensive, blame their customers, make excuses and shout down critics.

Feedback from customers is vital in learning how to improve service. Too many companies pay lip-service to it, soliciting feedback which they do not acknowledge and appear to do little with.

Getting genuine, objective feedback can be an exciting process and should not be limited to one approach only. There is a vast reservoir of methods available for use. These include:

1. Going out of your way yourself to meet your customers and find out what they think and feel about your organization, its products and service.
2. Employing market research companies to obtain feedback in a systematic and analytical way.
3. The use of customer comment cards and short questionnaires.
4. Customer surveys (for example, sent by mailshot).
5. Careful analyses of unsolicited complaints and compliments.
6. Listening to your staff about their experiences with customers and their suggestions in relation to them.

Generally, senior executives must develop an ethos within the organization where feedback is encouraged, reviewed and given high value.

Additionally, senior executives must develop processes which facilitate, within and beyond the organization, the acquisition of such feedback.

Senior executives must be seen not only to welcome feedback, but more importantly, act upon it. Communicating the action taken in response to such feedback is of paramount importance to secure both customer and employee goodwill.

It is a matter of placing exceptionally high value on what customers and front-line employees say. It is a matter of recognizing that such feedback is vital to the future success of the business.

Finding time for reviewing feedback (and taking follow-up action) thus becomes a high priority and critical task for all managers and their teams. The equation is simple. A customer who has a bad experience will have an alienation factor of between −1 and −10. Failing to deal effectively with the complaint will exacerbate the problem and lead to an alienation factor of between −10 and −50. Conversely, an effective (positive) and active (repairing) response can result in a satisfaction factor of between +1 and +50.

Customers who provide feedback, whether solicited or unsolicited, need some recognition and appreciation of their efforts. Why take the trouble to write to or telephone the offending company if there is no visible response from the organization?

It is essential that whatever shape or form the feedback takes there is some immediate acknowledgement of it. At worst, this should be a card. Best, however, is a personalized letter, telephone call or even meeting, to explain what action is being taken in response to the feedback.

Bland, stereotyped, word-processed responses are barely adequate. They merely signal to the customer how unimportant his or her feedback is perceived to be by the company. It leaves the impression that such feedback is routine and insignificant amongst the vast volume of complaints received.

Sometimes the feedback might appear trivial, but what is trivial to a senior executive might be critically important to a customer. Much of customer service is about getting the little things right and to that extent, nothing is too trivial for the attention of a senior executive. Trivial incidents often reveal much bigger problems.

Involving the customer in providing feedback is an important way of securing the customer's long-term commitment to the company. Customers like to be liked by the organization whose services they use, they like to feel important and valued, they like to feel their viewpoint is welcomed and highly considered.

Some personal challenges

- List out all the channels of feedback from your customers (internal or external) to you.
- How seriously do you consider such feedback?
- How frequently do you sit down with your team and review such feedback?

- What conscious efforts have you taken over recent months to improve the channels of feedback?
- What initiative can you take today to secure better feedback and make better use of it?

REMEMBER:
Never ever criticize the customers who give you feedback, no matter how disagreeable it is.

RETAIL COMPANY - DIRECT FEEDBACK

'In my company we have a rule that if a letter of a customer is addressed personally to an executive, whether it be the Chairman, Chief Executive or whoever, then that person will reply personally. If a customer goes out of the way to find the name of the executive to write to, then the least thing that executive can do is reply personally.

'Of course, if the Chairman ends up with hundreds of letters that is going to reveal to him that we have a major problem in the organization.'

23

Teamwork

'It always takes more than one person to provide a superb service to the customer.'

To achieve customer service excellence, the person serving at the front-line is dependent on a large number of other people.

In a supportive, customer-caring organization, an inordinate amount of time, energy and resource is directed towards front-line people, to ensure they have the appropriate tools for the job, the appropriate training, the appropriate documentation to hand, the appropriate environment and the appropriate counselling and advice when things go wrong.

In such an organization (see Figure 23.1), all the teams face towards the front-line interaction with the customer, whereas in a traditional, hierarchical organization (the traditional pyramid) everyone faces in the reverse direction – upwards towards senior management and the chief executive.

One of the key tasks of any manager, therefore, is to develop superb 'team approach', whereby the group of individuals in the team share the same set of values, beliefs and direction (vision) in relation to serving the customer. Lack of team cohesion through a lack of shared values can have an adverse impact on the customer. For example, senior bosses who set very rigid rules often put staff in a situation where they either alienate the customer or have to break the rules.

The successful manager will get his or her team together to iron out such conflicts, and to resolve some of the silly problems which

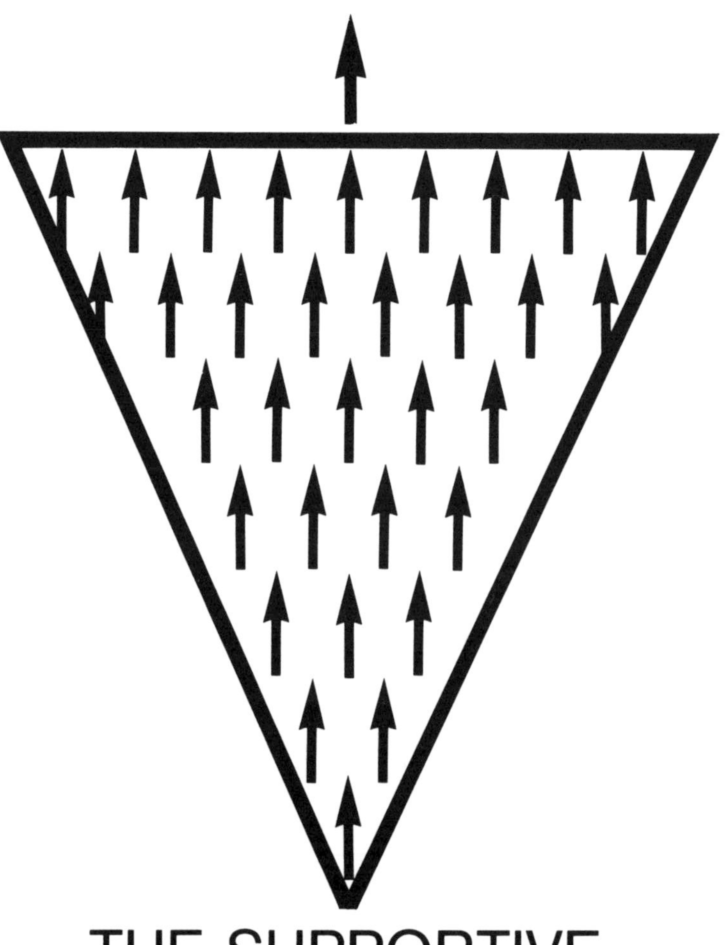

Figure 23.1 Teams directed towards the customer

BMW - TEAMWORK

'In our Service Reception area if a queue suddenly forms, the General Manager, or any other member of the team available will go to the counter to help out the receptions and alleviate the queue.'

BMW Dealership, Maidenhead

irritate and frustrate customers. By developing the team approach, the manager will create an ethos of 'everyone helping each other'. With such an approach, telephones and correspondence do not go unanswered and customer problems get fixed no matter who the customer comes into contact with. There is no question of 'Sally is away, can you call back Thursday and she'll deal with your problem then', but more a question of 'Don't worry, I'll sort it out even though Sally's away.'

By developing a cohesive team, whether it be at Branch, District, Area or Regional level, the manager creates an environment whereby any one person can turn to a colleague for help and advice. If a problem suddenly arises at the front-line, anyone available will 'muck in' to help.

In the absence of teamwork, a culture of divisiveness, self-interest, individualism, cynicism, internal politics and prima donna-like behaviour will develop. The resultant lack of co-operation and bad feelings will inevitably have a repercussion through to the customer who will see inefficiency and disinterest.

The teamwork approach should extend beyond the immediate boundaries of accountability to the furthest corners of the organization. Team work means the finance department working closely with sales to ensure that refunds are quickly and effectively processed. It means distribution working closely with sales to ensure that orders are delivered on time and there are no shorts. It means personnel facilitating an effective recruitment process so that there is minimum delay in appointing front-line people. Overall, it means recognition that everyone is part of both a small team and a larger organization team and that whatever the team there is only one aim – to satisfy the customer.

Some personal challenges

- To what degree does your team share the same set of values, beliefs and directions with respect to customer service?
- List down the steps you have taken over recent months to develop and reinforce the team approach.
- Produce an outline team development plan with a specific focus on customer service, discuss it with your team and implement it soon.

REMEMBER:
Teamwork is synonymous with leadership, your leadership in achieving *incredible customer service*.

24

Caring for employees

'You cannot separate customer care from employee care.'

Customers are often inadvertently made to feel bad by employees who feel bad about their company and their bosses. Their disgruntlement shows through in their disinterest and 'can't be bothered' attitudes.

'If the company doesn't bother about me, why should I bother about the company (and its customers)?'

The converse is true. Employees who feel valued and cared for will value their customers and care for them.

Amazingly, many managers neglect to care effectively for their people. Often, they don't even know or understand what care is.

Care is not a soft welfare-oriented concept. It is caring to get the best out of your team by doing your best for them. It is caring to define the best and develop the best. It is caring for high standards in every aspect of your business and personnel practice, for example, high standards of training, employee communications and welfare facilities.

It is caring to ensure that your front-line people have the best tools to do the job and are provided with up-to-date information (price lists, sales literature, new product data) so that they can be effective in dealing with customers.

It is caring to ensure that your people have a comfortable environment within which they can perform effectively. The probability is that if they are comfortable they will make their customers comfortable.

It is caring for them so much that you give them regular feedback about their performance so that they know where they stand with you.

It is caring to encourage them, to support them, to take an interest in them. Caring is about going out of your way to praise them for exceptional work, as well as perhaps biting your tongue when you don't always agree with what they say or do.

It is caring to give them time, to listen to them, to counsel them. Nothing devalues employees more than when a boss fails to find time for them.

It is caring to chat to them about their customers and the level of service provided, the problems encountered.

It is caring to ensure employees don't work excessive hours and burn themselves out. (Many bosses set an incredibly bad example by working crazy hours.) The really caring bosses insist on their people taking leave and going home on time. They know that excessive hours at work can render people ineffective.

Caring for employees is total care, a total care exhibited by line managers and not left to personnel.

Caring is not being soft, is not turning a blind eye to ineptness. Caring is not about pouring syrup over people nor buttering them up when you want something. Caring is all about being open and honest when a person's performance deteriorates. Caring is about confronting important (but not trivial) problems.

It is caring to give your front-line people real accountability – real scope for making decisions, for developing within their jobs, for taking initiatives.

It is caring to learn together about mistakes made.

Caring for employees is as much a way of life as is caring for customers. The two are essentially synonymous.

Some personal challenges

- Do you really care for your people? If so, how do you show it?
- In what practical way does that care relate to customer care?
- Find out whether your people really believe you care for them. You might be surprised at the answer.

REMEMBER:
The level of customer care is a mere reflection of what you care for, and for whom.

25

Customer service as a performance measure

'Employees must be able to relate the corporate service goals, as well as their department goals, to their own contribution, and consequently receive feedback about their own performance.'

Exhortations to improve customer service do not get very far. More important is the provision of feedback to people in the organization about their own performance in contributing to the company's customer service goals.

It is the failure by management to do this that can devalue a company's approach to customer service, that can engender cynicism and disbelief, that can reduce declarations of intent about customer service to a mere set of words on paper.

In establishing performance measures by way of personal targets or individual objectives it is imperative that clearly defined goals and standards are set up for every employee, together with monitoring procedures.

There should be no ambiguity about these goals. Ideally each employee should be involved in setting the goals and committed to achieving them. Obtaining a clear focus on individual goals enables employees to appreciate how important their contribution is to the company's success.

The individual goals must be simple, measurable, and ideally, not number more than three or four. For example if the corporate 'first-step' goal is to achieve a 95 per cent telephone response within five seconds then this can be applied to every supervisor in every department. Each supervisor will have to ensure that telephones in his or her section are covered at all times and encourage staff to answer each other's phones when people are away.

Independent checking on response times will need to be carried out, section by section, to provide a monitoring service to supervisors. This will provide an opportunity for department managers to give their supervisors praise when the goal is achieved, or discuss shortfalls when it is not. Supervisors, in turn, will need to involve their front-line people in the same way.

Establishing simple performance measures across the organization, together with effective monitoring will enable managers to progress improvements to achieve priority goals.

Other goals, such as positive employee attitudes, can equally well be set and measured, both internally and externally. Carefully designed surveys can be used for this purpose. When the survey reveals exceptionally friendly, warm and helpful attitudes, there is an opportunity for managers to provide encouraging and appreciative feedback. Conversely, disinterested, negative, 'can't be bothered' attitudes reveal morale problems requiring management attention.

When clear performance measures are set, employees gain confidence. They will 'know where they stand' and will not have to suffer the uncertainty of responding to the whims of unpredictable bosses. When clear performance measures are set, employees can deploy all their energies in one or two specific directions, which they know are vital for success. Furthermore they know that their contribution will be recognized and appreciated by the bosses. This cannot be the case when clear goals are not set.

Without clear performance measures, any positive feedback can often appear patronizing, whimsical, false and inconsistent, whereas any negative feedback can often appear arbitrary, trivial, reactionary, inconsequential and, most importantly, unfair.

Some personal challenges

- How do you measure up to your own personal customer service performance goals?
- Do you ever review your own customer service performance with your boss? If not, and you really believe customer service is of paramount importance, go and initiate a review now.
- Have you developed performance measures for your team and every individual within it? If not, do so right now.
- Ensure you give regular feedback on the performance attained by way of these measures.

REMEMBER:
To manage customer service you have to measure it.

26

Recruiting for customer service

'It starts before they start. If you are looking for* incredible customer service, *look for people who can provide it.'

The reason why customer service is often so poor is that managers do not recruit for it in the first place. People often get selected solely on the basis of their professional or technical expertise, their business capability, sales record, by sheer dint of muscle and intellect, or simply by being available.

Too few recruiters look for people with the ability to relate to customers, to understand their needs, to take initiatives on their behalf. They do not look for these qualities, because customer service is not deeply valued within the organization. At best, it is seen as a superficial aspect of the company's business, but not as a key factor for the recruitment and selection process.

The evidence is to be found in many retail stores, with staff who are totally devoid of any real interest in the customer, and staff who blindly stick to the rules and frequently lack initiative or any semblance of product knowledge.

Incredible customer service must therefore start with the recruitment and selection process. The job specification and subsequently the person specification, must emphasize the exceptional value placed on customer service.

Sincerity, honesty, humility, modesty, charm, communication skills, listening skills, sensitivity, understanding, tolerance, pleasing personality and initiative are some of the many qualities that should be spelt out in the person specification for the job, and looked for critically in the selection process.

Failure to identify and confirm these qualities when recruiting will inevitably lead to poor customer service.

Many of these qualities are not directly measurable and therefore do not always show through during interview, when candidates often fail to reveal their true colours, sometimes hideously misrepresenting themselves or purposely misleading the interviewer.

Interviews are invariably artificial and false. They can be a process of mutual seduction if one is not careful, and such seduction is based on illusion, pose, facade and front. Such are the cosmetics of selection.

To delve deep, to discover whether the candidate is genuinely customer-oriented will involve much time and many people. No one manager can make an effective judgement. Selecting for *incredible customer service* means involving as many members of the team as possible, as well as available colleagues and personnel professionals. They should have an opportunity to make their own assessment of the short-list candidates, for in doing so they will elicit and highlight different facets of the interviewee's skills, attitudes and orientation.

It might well be a long haul, it might well be time consuming, but if the interviewee proves acceptable to all the team players, managers and professional advisers, then there is a high probability that he or she will prove acceptable to the customer. If any one of the interviewers should object to a candidate because of perceived limitations, then this person should be vetoed. It is not worth taking the risk of hiring people who are unacceptable to other members of the team.

People tend to behave differently during an interview, trying to simulate what they think the interviewers want. The selection skill is to get underneath the simulated behaviour and discover the real person, ideally a person who enjoys being with customers, looking after them, talking with them and who, crucially, believes customers are important. The greater the number of people involved in the selection process the greater the probability of discovering the real person and making the correct recruitment decision.

Some recruiters like to use certain techniques such as graphology, aptitude and psychometric tests to provide additional information about the interviewee. From the author's experience many of these techniques are contrived – and those interviewees who excel at them are not necessarily those who will excel in the real work situation.

The key in any selection situation is to get inside the real person – rather than just get a reflection from the surface. To achieve this requires interview after interview, using different interviewers who will inevitably perceive the interviewee in different ways. The team of interviewers should then get together to present their assessments and views and advise the recruiting manager on the most appropriate candidate.

Some personal challenges

- What do you look for when you are recruiting?
- How important is customer service orientation in your selection process?
- Re-evaluate your approach to recruitment and selection and place an even higher value on customer orientation.

REMEMBER:
You are recruiting for the customer.

27

Training for customer service

'Those who claim they have nothing to learn, have the most to learn, especially about customer service. Training for improvement should be ongoing and applicable to all.'

The final test of *incredible customer service* cannot be passed without everyone in the organization undergoing regular training on the subject. There is always something new to learn, or something to relearn about how customer service relates to their jobs.

Training is all about learning and development, it does not therefore have to be confined to the classroom. Regular workshops, seminars or even two-hour 'teach-ins' conducted by the boss can serve well in leading people through a thought-process to review their current approach to customer service and how it can be improved. (Unless you are completely close-minded you must accept that there is always scope for improvement.)

Training enables participants to sit back and take an in-depth look at their existing skills, attitudes, practices and overall approach in contributing towards achieving incredible service. It enables people to come up with new ideas, provide feedback and learn from each other.

While there is no magic formula to be taught, customer service training does enable people to 'regenerate' their belief in providing exceptional service to their customers, as well as restore their motivation for doing so. Training helps them regain their personal pride in achieving superb customer service, and also creates an awareness that the company really does value their hour-by-hour efforts to keep the customer happy.

Training gives people confidence – confidence in the company's real commitment to achieving *incredible customer service* and confidence in themselves towards achieving it. Such encouragement is highly motivational.

If achieving incredible service really is an overriding obsession in the company, then no single person (director, senior manager, supervisor or front-line employee) should be allowed to escape the regular events set up to learn more about customer service.

When it comes to budgeting, senior managers must ensure that sufficient funds are allocated for this purpose. Whilst regular sessions can be run on site by experienced and inspirational managers, there is a need, from time to time, to extract people from their current environment and send them to a pleasant hotel or training centre to gain a fresh perspective on customer service. There is also a need to bring in experts from other organizations, who can lend their views, experience and ideas to the benefit of the in-house group. Independent facilitators will also be required from time to time to stimulate debate and lift the horizons of the participants. All this will cost money and should be provided for either in central or department budgets.

The danger with much in-house training is that it becomes inbred, divorced from reality, 'academic' and, worst of all, propagandizing. Many in-house trainers are rejects from the line who do no better than expostulate theoretical concepts which the participants find difficult to relate to in practice. The skill in training for customer service is to relate concept to reality, to bridge the gap between current practices and future ideals. This is where the skill of a high quality facilitator comes in. Such a person will also have the capability of eliminating any cynicism and defeatism and convert participants into a motivated team which actually believes it can make improvements on customer service. Such cynicism and defeatism is deep-rooted in many organizations today.

Put another way, quality customer service requires quality training. It cannot be done on the cheap by second-rate instructors. Trainees in today's organization require inspiration and stimulation. Companies who are passionate about customer service will invest accordingly.

Some personal challenges

- Analyse the training needs for your organization in relation to customer care. Then develop a strategy to meet these needs. The strategy might well include a number of core training events relating to:
  - Attitude
  - Skills
  - Organization systems and knowledge.

  An example of a training strategy is given in Figure 27.1, followed by an example programme of a typical workshop (Figure 27.2).
- Go ahead and initiate these training events using the services of central training where appropriate.
- In any event, ensure that all your team participate in the Customer Service Workshops within the next six months. Ensure that the workshop has the highest quality facilitator and is conducted in a pleasant environment conducive to quality thinking.
- Repeat the workshops regularly.
- In the interim, conduct your own two-hour teach-ins on Customer Service with the team.

REMEMBER:
Learning how to improve customer service is a lifelong pursuit.

CUSTOMER SERVICE TRAINING STRATEGY CORE COMPONENTS

ATTITUDE	SKILLS	ORGANIZATION SYSTEMS/KNOWLEDGE
PURPOSE To get people involved in 'customer service' and develop positive attitudes towards it.	PURPOSE To help employees develop the skills necessary to achieve customer service excellence.	PURPOSE To help employees acquire the required knowledge about the organization, its systems and approach to achieve customer service excellence.
PARTICIPANTS Everyone in organization (15 people at a time)	PARTICIPANTS Various groups according to needs analysis	PARTICIPANTS Various groups according to needs analysis
EVENTS 1 One day workshops (see example programme following page) 2 Follow-up workshops (after 6 months – half a day) 3 Regular half day workshops on customer service	EVENTS (Based on needs analysis) 1 Relationship skills – 2 days 2 Telephone skills – 1 day 3 Letterwriting skills – 1 day 4 Managing for customer service – 2 days 5 'Taking the initiative' in customer service – 1 day	EVENTS (Based on needs analysis) 1 Induction – 1 day (company knowledge, organization, who's who, etc.) 2 Customer service policies – 1 day (compliments, complaints, refunds, accountabilities, etc.) 3 Customer service systems – 1 day (computers, ordering, invoicing, after-sales servicing, information, etc.)

Figure 27.1 Example of a training strategy

WORKSHOP PROGRAMME

One day workshop

CUSTOMER SERVICE EXCELLENCE
'from principles to practice'
led by
Jilly Smith

Company Training Centre, Friday 9 July

PURPOSE

To develop the team's approach to achieving the company vision of total quality and customer service excellence

To highlight issues that need to be addressed in relation to the vision

To identify and commit to actions for achieving this vision

AGENDA

- Introduction
- 'Visions of excellence'
  Talk by Jilly Smith
  followed by discussion
- 'The company vision in practice'
  Small groups
- 'Issues to be addressed in achieving the vision'
  Open forum sessions:
- 'A plan of departmental action'
  Small groups
- Presentations to Director
- Conclusions

TIMETABLE

9.00am Arrive/coffee
9.30am Start
11.00am Coffee
12.30pm Lunch
1.30pm Restart
3.00pm Tea
5.00pm Finish

casual dress please!

Figure 27.2 Example programme of a typical workshop

28

Rewarding excellent service

'Success in achieving excellent customer service must be celebrated and rewarded.'

A sense of achievement can be a reward in itself. Recognition by others of that achievement is an even bigger reward and is often best expressed through celebration.

What personnel experts often fail to see is that the 'process of rewarding' can be just as important as the actual reward itself.

The reward (or award) does not need to be of intrinsic value. Greater value can be placed on the way in which the reward is handed over.

A cheque for £100 sent impersonally through the post is far less effective as a reward than £100 spent on a celebration at which an intrinsically worthless piece of paper (a certificate) is handed out in style.

Deciding upon a reward is a creative opportunity for a manager to demonstrate appreciation in a unique way. The reward process will be an expression of the manager's personality and effectively be a token of his or her recognition of a team member's achievement.

The reward does not necessarily have to be formally presented. Informal celebrations can be equally meaningful. Taking the team up the pub on a Friday lunch-time after some excellent customer service can have as much impact as a major event. Each manager has to decide his or her style of rewarding in relation to the team and the type of achievement.

The key principle for any manager is to recognize the importance of rewarding excellent customer service. There are many innovative ways of putting the principle into practice and these can vary from manager to manager (see below).

As soon as the reward process develops into a routine, the process becomes devalued. Spontaneous expression in celebrating success is far better than a mechanistic process in which the organization is trawled for an 'employee of the month', and the reluctant victim exposed to the ritual of a hand-shake with the Managing Director and the full glare of the company newspaper.

THINGS TO REWARD	**WAYS OF REWARDING**
Complimentary letters	**Cakes**
Top of the league in surveys	**Customer service award evenings**
Service improvements	**Day out at the races**
Achievement of specific goals	**Books or book tokens**
Exceptional service stories (putting yourself out)	**Chinese meal for the team**
	Weekend break for a couple
Lots of little extras	**A personal letter from the Chief Executive**
Great ideas which are implemented	**Mickey Mouse prizes**
Bottom line results	**Wall plaques**
etc. etc . . .	**etc. etc . . .**

To reward successful employees and teams, there must be an element of surprise, of excitement, of elation. The process must be fun, inspirational and motivating, as opposed to a bureaucratic chore run by personnel people.

The higher the value of the reward, the more important it is to ensure that the process for determining who receives the reward is based on fairness and objectivity. Achievers who must miss out year in and year out can justifiably feel aggrieved when they see their recently appointed counterparts flying off to Paris or Rome for running the best 'Customer Service Branch' in the region.

Far better to keep the value of the reward low, and broaden the net to include as many real achievers as possible. The benefit of investing in the process, as well as the reward, is that many more people can participate in the celebration than just the achievers themselves. In this way, the value of customer service is reinforced.

No manager need wait for the company to adopt a formalized approach to reward customer service excellence. The best managers just get off their backsides and reward their people in the most appropriate way, they know instinctively the importance of doing it. For them, it is not necessary to have central direction or finely tuned personnel policies to reward their people effectively.

Some personal challenges

- By waiting for corporate initiatives you might wait for ever and fail totally in motivating your people to serve the customers well. Far better you do your own thing and initiate your own reward process today.
- To avert the cynics, the constrainers and the cost-conscious 'can't doers' in the organization, all you need to do is develop an approach which incurs minimal expense and time. You shouldn't even be afraid of dipping your hand into your own pocket – that's one of the privileges you have as a boss – to give yourself to your team!

REMEMBER:
The reward is a reflection of the value you place on customer service and your people's contribution to it.

29

Continuous monitoring

'Standards can only be improved by monitoring existing levels of customer service.'

Without any form of measure you cannot know how well you are doing in serving the customer.

One of the key thrusts of this book is that to pass the final test of achieving *incredible customer service*, specific goals and standards must be established and striven for throughout the organization. Such are the fourteen key goals set out in the first part of this book.

Progress in achieving these goals must be monitored, whether it be on a daily, weekly, monthly or quarterly basis.

For example, it is no good striving to achieve a two-day document response unless every single person in the organization has their own document responses monitored (if necessary on a random sample basis) and provided with feedback. If the company decides to shoot for such a goal as a first step in improving customer service (and thus profitability) it is just as important that the document response time in the Chief Executive's office is monitored as that of the enquiry clerk in accounts or the recruitment administrator in personnel.

Too often, companies set out their customer service stall with fuzzy declarations of intent which have no real impact on the actual operation of the business nor on the delivery of service to the customer. The only way to achieve progress is to specify exactly what is required in terms of customer service and then monitor whether or not this requirement is being met throughout the organization.

More difficult to monitor, but equally important to do so, is employee attitudes. The disinterested, disenchanted, front-line employee can be one of the biggest turn-offs in any customer service situation.

In developing an organization-wide customer service monitoring process, it is worth focusing attention on the key customer contact points for the organization. These might well include:

- Sales counters
- Receptions
- Cashiers
- Switchboards and telephones
- Accounts department
- General enquiries
- Service providers (engineers, delivery people, drivers etc.)

For each of these contact points there should be a small set of key customer service goals (say three), against which each person (or team) is monitored. (See Figure 29.1.)

Each person in the respective team should be aware of these key goals and receive feedback on their performance in relation to them.

The monitoring process should not be unduly bureaucratic. A simple process of random checks and occasional surveys should be adequately followed by a simple report back, by the manager, to the people involved. The report back should be in summary written form, coupled with a face-to-face chat, at which due praise can be given, or opportunities for improvement discussed.

Monitoring customer service does not mean monitoring every customer service contact.

In addition to random checks and surveys, other monitoring

KEY TARGETS TO BE MONITORED (examples)

Teams:	GOAL 1	GOAL 2	GOAL 3
Sales counters	Positive attitudes	5 min. queuing	Product knowledge (no delays by having to defer to others to get information on product)
Cash-tills	Positive attitudes	5 min. queuing	Accuracy (no till errors)
Switchboard	Positive attitudes	5 sec. responses	Pro-active communications (no customers kept hanging on)
Accounts (enquiries)	Positive attitudes	2 day responses	Accuracy and clarity (customer files up-to-date, easily accessible – enquiries answered promptly, accurately and clearly)
General enquiries (Reception)	Positive attitudes	All waiting visitors communicated with every 5 minutes. All waiting visitors offered tea/coffee	Company knowledge (no delays trying to find out who's who in organization)
Service providers	Positive attitudes	Always arrive on time	Pro-active communications (help customer understand product delivered or installed, advise customer how to correct faults, obtain service etc.)
MONITORING > TECHNIQUE >	**SURVEYS CUSTOMER F/BACK**	**RANDOM CHECKS**	**SURVEYS CUSTOMER F/BACK**

Figure 29.1 Examples of key customer service goals

devices – such as customer questionnaires and unsolicited letters – can be used to monitor service levels. The ultimate monitoring test, of course, is the bottom line and how well or otherwise each person, team or unit is doing in terms of attracting business. Monitored levels of customer satisfaction should always be linked to levels of profitability.

Some personal challenges

- If you really believe customer service is important, make sure you have established some meaningful measures of it and some simple methods of monitoring it in relation to the measures.
- Ensure all your team is committed to achieving the goals to be measured and is interested in receiving the feedback from the monitoring process.
- Never use the information collected as a means of threatening your people, if from time to time they fall below standard. Always use it as a source of encouragement and potential celebration.

REMEMBER:
The monitoring process provides a focus for you to improve your approach to customer service.

30

Constant improvement

'Customer service is a moving horizon, the high standards of today can be the low standards of a few years time. Constant improvement is a necessity.'

Incredible customer service can only be achieved by a continual quest for improvement. Which business traveller today would be happy with a hotel room which didn't have a television, a trouser-press, beverage facilities and a private en suite bathroom and toilet? Yet it wasn't so many years ago that the norm was to walk along the corridor to the toilet, to watch television with other guests in the lounge and to have to go to the bar or restaurant to obtain a coffee. Perhaps in a few years time, every business person will expect a fax, cable television, desk-top computer and other hi-tech facilities in his or her hotel room.

Constant improvement is synonymous with unlimited opportunity. Complacency soon sets in when you believe in the adequacy of your current service provision, when you delude yourself that the high level of achievement today will yield customer satisfaction tomorrow.

You have to believe that there is always opportunity for improvement. It had always been the case and always will be – so are you seeking it with respect to customer service in your specific area of responsibility?

As competitive pressures intensify and the customer increasingly focuses on service, in addition to product, the requirement for improvement becomes critical in sustaining the long term success of a business. Failure to improve will result in a perceived drop in standards relative to the competition. Organizations that fail to improve on customer service will breed disinterested staff more interested in the comfort of the status quo than the excitement of progress.

The quest for improvement is a motivator. It provides an exceptional challenge for everyone in the organization, it provides an opportunity to be creative, to generate new ideas, to take initiatives no matter how small. It provides an opportunity to go home with the knowledge that today's customer was even more satisfied than yesterday's.

Customer service provides an excellent focus for what the organization is all about, it provides an opportunity to create a learning environment in which everyone can develop and achieve more.

Fundamentally, the quest for constant improvement is an attitude of mind that should prevail in every team member in the organization.

It is the absence of that attitude that lets many companies down, that turns many customers off. 'This is the way we do it, this is the way we have always done it and this is the way you will have it.' In the end, the customer gets fed up with being force-fitted into the company's approach, for example having to put it into writing when others do it by telephone.

Customers can forgive mistakes, systems failures and even defective products. What they find less easy to forgive is persistent negative attitudes where the staff seem disinterested, never put themselves out and rarely get things done properly or on time.

The achievement of many of the goals specified in the first part of this book is dependent on people with exceptionally positive attitudes towards the customer and service.

Attitudes deteriorate unless reinforced, nourished, refreshed, stimulated. That is why the process of management is so critical in achieving the highest standards of customer service. It is an on-going challenge to managers. There are always opportunities to improve upon attitudes, to prevent them slipping into defeatism, cynicism and helplessness. Ideally, the person interacting with the customer is one who feels he or she has maximum opportunity for satisfying that customer.

To achieve such positive attitudes, a manager has to invest an inordinate amount of time, effort and resource in getting the people thing right in his or her team. It requires inspiration and enthusiasm on the manager's part as well as a real commitment to training and development.

Ideally, the manager creates a culture where everyone wants to improve. It is a climate in which the manager is humble enough to admit mistakes, deficiencies and shortcomings, and is open and honest to admit that he or she can improve too.

- One additional smile is an improvement.
- One small initiative can lead to an improvement.
- One short word by way of pro-active communication can be an improvement.
- One little piece of positive feedback to a hard-pressed front-line employee can trigger some improvement.

The opportunities for improving customer service are endless.

Your challenge is to seize those opportunities. If you don't someone else will and you will be assigned to the ranks of the mediocre!

Some personal challenges

- Make one improvement in customer service today.
- Make another tomorrow.
- Make five by the weekend and twenty by the end of the month.

REMEMBER:
Incredible customer service results from continuous improvement.

Part 3

SOME PRACTICAL STEPS

'Customer service is a practice, not a theory.'

In the first two parts of this book, the emphasis has been on establishing some fundamental tests for *incredible customer service*, and on the management process for achieving the required goals. In every section there have been some personal challenges to you, the reader, as to how you will put all this into practice.

In Part Three some of these practical steps are summarized. They are all fairly basic and do not require a vast amount of resources to implement. However, they are essential in passing that final test of *incredible customer service*.

31

Customer service notebook

Taking notes of your observations about customer service in practice is a great discipline for focusing your mind on improvements. As a manager, you should also encourage your team to take notes and then take interest in the observations they record. Using a customer service notebook increases awareness and catalyses new ideas.

In a team meeting, it is fun to compare notes, discuss them and chew over the implications. The notebook itself should not be part of any formal bureaucratic process, but more an aide memoire in a personal and team development process to improve customer service. The notebook should remain personal and no attempt should be made to publish or circulate its contents.

The customer service notebook is essentially a prompt, a prompt for team reviews and for action you can take personally.

The human memory is incredibly fallible. What is fresh in your mind now will become stale in an hour's time and forgotten tomorrow. The customer service notebook provides you with an opportunity to trap, whilst fresh, a whole range of observations about customer service in practice. It doesn't matter how minor or major the observation is, if you are making a mental note, then make a written note too.

Why not spend an hour walking around your organization observing customer service in practice? Make a note of anything that strikes you as being exceptionally good or exceptionally poor. Also, get out and about and make a note of what your competitors are doing in terms of customer service.

Use your comparative notes as a focus for a team discussion on improving customer service.

EXAMPLE - NOTEBOOK

Tuesday 8 June

09.00am	Rang Jill, my secretary, from airport. No answer. Put down phone after two minutes.
09.04am	Rang Jill, my secretary, from airport. Line continually engaged.
09.10am	Eventually got through. Our Director had called her around to help out on an urgent task.
10.00am	Took a look at car park. Need to improve signage to visitors' bay. Also too much litter in car park. Discuss both with team.
10.02am	Long queues in reception. Seems to be the norm nowadays. Discuss with Dick Brown.
10.15am	Two customer complaints in in-tray about late deliveries and inability to get through to Distribution on telephone. Discuss with Ben Jefferson.
10.16am	Complimentary letter about the way Mary Godstone put herself out to deliver an urgent order. Write to Mary Godstone, copy Ben Jefferson.
11.40am	Popped down to reception and chatted to a couple of customers. 'They like our products, they hate our queues.'

32

Customer service workshops

The term 'workshop' is just management jargon for getting together a group of people to work through problems and issues of common interest. But it's appropriate jargon, as a workshop invariably is hard work. To get a disparate group of individuals to think deeply about the past, present and future and reach a degree of consensus on action to be taken, is incredibly difficult.

A workshop helps focus minds and challenges perceptions and priorities that are taken for granted by busy people who rarely have time to think or have their view subjected to intense debate.

Use an external facilitator if need be (the excellent ones are really expensive), but the key is to ensure that the workshop has clear objectives and is chaired in a way that enables open and honest discussion, as well as providing direction towards the objectives.

If, as a boss, you decide to facilitate a customer service workshop yourself, you must ensure that your views do not dominate and that you do not suppress the views and feelings of your team - no matter how unpalatable and disagreeable you find them. Fairness, independence and, from time to time, firm handling are the key criteria for a successful facilitator. Facilitation is exhausting and skilled work requiring immense powers of concentration and understanding to guide your group to its own conclusions on what needs to be done.

By using a workshop to reach deep into your team's minds about customer service, you will create an excellent opportunity to develop and reinforce a shared set of values, beliefs and direction about customer service in your part of the world. A successful customer workshop will develop renewed commitment to achieving a vision of customer service as well as motivate the participants to achieve it.

The best workshops involve a residential stay so that the team can relax and socialize together over dinner. Two days are ideal to get some real, clear thinking underway. A bare minimum would be half-a-day, finishing or starting with lunch.

Those teams that do not invest their time and funds in workshops often get lost in the routines of day-to-day business. Customer service will inevitably suffer when people get into automatic mode and take everything for granted.

Progress on customer service can only be made when the organization's approach, its systems and the way its people think is put up for challenge from time to time and fresh minds brought to bear on the totality of the business.

The workshop provides an excellent opportunity to make such progress.

Get your team together soon and organize a date for a customer service workshop within the next three months!

33

Goal setting

To achieve an incredible level of customer service, specific goals must be set for progress to be made.

These goals must be:

- Few in number;
- Simple and clear;
- Measurable;
- Critical for the success of your business;
- An integral part of your overall customer service vision.

You should select two or three of the goals represented by the fourteen tests in the first part of this book. Ensure that the goals relate to your customer service vision (which you should establish in the first place if you don't have one).

Before committing your organization to the achievement of these goals, discuss them with your team, obtaining their views, as well as their commitment.

Look at the feasibility of achieving the goals within a given time-span. In doing so, ask yourself the following questions:

1. Is any additional resource or investment required to achieve these goals?
2. If yes, what will be the long-term benefit to the organization in achieving these goals (in other words, your estimate of the bottom-line impact)?
3. Are you confident you can put a persuasive case to your own boss for such resources and investment?

4. Given support from the organization, do you and your team genuinely believe you can achieve these goals?
5. What is your back-up plan if you don't get support for the resource required to achieve these goals?
6. Finally, ask yourself this: Is additional resource really the answer to your quest for improving customer service? Are there any goals you can set and achieve without additional resource, for example relating to attitudinal change?

Having answered these questions, re-examine the feasibility of achieving these goals by having your approach to them tested and re-tested by your team, acting as devil's advocates.

Then test the goals once again by involving other people in your organization, perhaps some of the supervisors and front-line people. Get them to discuss how the goals might be applied to their jobs, and to suggest how the goals might be refined or developed. By involving as many people as possible, you maximize the opportunities for commitment and ownership of the achievement process.

If, after this process of involvement and consultation, you and your team are still confident that you can achieve these goals, then go ahead.

Ensure you give feedback to all the others involved in the process as to what the final goals are and how they relate to the vision. Furthermore, ensure that the goals are expressed in a simple, meaningful way that everyone can relate to.

Finally, set up some clear measures for monitoring progress. Pull all this together in the form of an action plan which you can use as a focus for progress reviews.

When undertaking the progress reviews it might well be that the goals set are insufficiently demanding and that you need to set more challenging ones to stretch your people. There are no absolutes in customer service, so there are always opportunities for doing better!

34

Audit trails

No matter how good the feedback you and your own people produce with regard to the standards of customer service you achieve, there will always be an element of subjectivity and bias.

The only way to overcome this is to initiate a regular and independent audit of customer service.

The two keys are regularity and independence.

A once-off audit of customer service in your area will merely reinforce your own self-delusions about how good or bad the service really is. A regular six-monthly audit will demonstrate a trend, and thereby reflect the excellence, or otherwise, of your efforts.

The audit should be simple, with a small number of parameters reflecting the critical goals you have set as a part of your long-term customer service vision.

There are a number of ways of ensuring the audit is independent:

- You can ask other departments in the company to provide people for a company team, to audit your department.
- You can spend money on using an external market survey company.
- You can set up a panel of customers to audit your service.
- You can use a combination of all three of these.

The method of the audit can vary enormously, depending on the nature of the company's products and services and your own areas of accountability. These methods might well include:

1. Random sampling, for example, of:
   - telephone response times
   - queueing times
   - delivery times
   - arrival times *vs* appointment times;
2. In-depth site, location or departmental inspections;
3. Analysis of compliments and complaints;
4. Analysis of completed customer questionnaires;
5. In-depth interviewing of customers;
6. Employee questionnaires;
7. In-depth interviewing of employees.

The audit should never be used as a 'fault-finding' process to establish blame for deficiencies in service.

Essentially, it should be an independent method of:

- measuring existing levels of service;
- monitoring the progress you and your people have made in implementing various customer service initiatives;
- identifying further areas for improvement.

35

Weekly reviews

Customer service is a topic that cannot wait for the next team meeting in a month's time or even later.

Customer service will always have an immediacy of fact and experience that will dissipate into a blur of mundane data and reports unless reviewed on a weekly basis.

The advantage of a weekly team review, which focuses solely on customer service, is that it reinforces the vital obsession you and your people have with achieving incredibly good customer service. Secondly, it enables you to explore recent experiences with customers while those experiences are still fresh in your mind (and notebook) and still significant. (Such significance can dangerously and quickly erode with the passage of time.) Furthermore, it enables you to take any necessary remedial action before it's too late.

Weekly reviews should be held throughout the organization. These should include half-hour sessions between front-line people and their supervisors, right through to half-hour sessions between directors and their senior managers.

Such reviews need have no agendas and should be lightly structured. All that should happen is a brief review of 'customer service happenings' during the last week. Any weekly data, reports, feedback, letters from customers and notebook observations should be reviewed. Each participant should feel free to contribute from their recent experience. Having brought into focus the experiences of the last week, the attention should then turn to the action necessary, during the coming week, to make improvements.

In a small, close-knit team, where there is a high degree of trust, formal written minutes will not be necessary. At best, the supervisor, manager or director in charge of the meeting should keep a handwritten note of items to be reviewed and actions to be taken. Other participants might well do the same to aid their contribution.

36

Out and about (customers' shoes)

There is no substitute for putting yourself in your customers' shoes from time to time, although there is no single way of doing this.

First of all, make a list of every conceivable interaction a customer might have directly or indirectly with people within your team.

For example:

1. Customers ringing you;
2. Customers ringing your sales people;
3. Coming into reception;
4. Handling an enquiry;
5. Actually providing a service to your customers;
6. Using one of your company's products;
7. Writing to you;
8. Writing to people in your department;
9. Attempting to buy one of your company's products;
10. Actually using your department's services;
11. Receiving invoices;
12. Receiving communications from you, your people or your company;
13. Interacting (touching base, seeking advice, making enquiries) with you or people in your department;
14. Surveying your customers.

Select one or more of the above interactions and try to envisage the ideal experience the customer should have. In other words, jot down the ideal standards you would like achieved.

Now go out and about with one or two of your closest neighbours, friends or family and try to 'simulate', as closely as you can, the selected interactions between a customer and your department.

Get your neighbour to ring up and ask for you, or one of your people and then honestly report on the experience.

Get a friend to come into reception and make enquiries about your company's range of products and services – and then tell you what happens.

Go and see some of your customers and ask them about their experiences with your company.

Get another neighbour to write to your department with a complaint or compliment (hopefully real) and gauge the response.

Go and visit a branch anonymously and experience what happens at the front-line.

Persuade another of your friends to attempt to buy one of your company's products (if it's a consumer product) and see how he or she feels about the ease, or otherwise, of doing so.

Talk to your customers about the invoices they receive. Are they accurate, are they sufficiently descriptive and informative? Are they too complicated, too unfriendly? Are they difficult to process (large computer sheets, difficult to file)?

Finally just get out and about on a regular basis and chat to your customers (internal or external) about the service they receive from you and your people.

Use the weekly reviews to assess the feedback. Furthermore, encourage everyone in your team to get out and about themselves, from time to time.

If, perchance, the feedback, albeit anecdotal and possibly a 'one-off', is negative, don't get negative and defensive yourself. Always listen carefully and take action.

The worst sin is to blame your customers for finding fault! You know how you feel when, as a customer, something goes wrong. So put yourselves as best you can into your customers' shoes today.

37

Brainstorming

Once in a while, get your team together and wipe your minds clean. Listen to some music together (tracks such as Tina Turner's 'Simply the Best'; Mozart's 'Piano Concerto K453'; Louis Armstrong's 'West End Blues'). A three to five minute airing will do.

Or meditate for five minutes. Read out some quotations from Lao Tzu. Get three members of your team to tell some amusing anecdote that has nothing to do with work. Or run a simple quiz.

When your minds have been wiped clean undertake a customer service brainstorm.

There are a number of ways of carrying this out. For example, you might give yourselves five minutes to list as many ideas as possible on how to please your customers even more. It doesn't matter how crazy or way-out the ideas are, at this stage they don't have to be feasible. Give a prize to the person who comes up with the longest list. Get each person to read out his or her list and give another prize to the person who raises the most laughs.

Then get down to the serious business. Go through the lists a second time and get the team to 'star' any particular ideas that appeal. Record these 'star' ideas on a flip chart. No discussion at this stage.

Now go through a process of evaluating the 'star' ideas into three categories:

1. Possible
2. Not sure
3. Impossible

Challenge yourselves on the second and third ideas. Never dismiss an idea prematurely.

Now break into syndicate groups and, from the first category, produce a five-star list of ideas you really want to pursue. Individual team members should then commit to championing each five-star idea through to fruition.

There are many other approaches to brainstorming. The key thing is get the team to think freely and produce as many ideas as possible. Always leave the evaluation process to the end. The purpose is to get people to eliminate from their minds all the constraints and prejudices about what cannot be done, but to think in a free-wheeling way what can be done.

Brainstorming can be an integral part of your customer service workshops or it can be a separate event, or it can be a spontaneous half-hour session during a routine team session.

Encouraging your team to think in a free-wheeling, brainstorming way will spark creative energies which elevate people out of the ruts of convention and tradition.

In poorly-led teams, ideas get stifled before they even surface. Creative people are discouraged by the 'Not invented here' syndrome, the 'We've seen it all before' disease, or the 'You remember what happened the last time we tried that' prejudice.

In well-led teams, ideas surface readily through the frequent release of creative energy and the encouraging of free-thinking and free-speech. Furthermore, people are given plenty of scope to pursue their ideas through to completion.

Finally, brainstorming costs no money and can be great fun.

So why not go brainstorming with your team today and identify five new ways of improving customer service?

38

Celebrating customer service successes

If you can't find any recent customer service successes to celebrate, it is because you are far from successful yourself.

No organization can survive or thrive without occasionally scoring some successes, minor or major, with their customers. As a superb boss, you should seize upon these successes and exploit them to the full, celebrating them with the very people who contributed to their achievement.

There is no better way to reinforce your team's obsession with customer service than celebrating successes in this area.

The celebration can be spontaneous for minor successes, or grand-slam events for continued successes or major improvements. A bottle of champagne after work for getting some new business, a team dinner at the local Chinese for getting into the top three in the company's league of customer service ratings, or a two-day conference – possibly abroad – when your revenues and profits have leaped ahead as a result of customer service improvements.

Don't turn a blind eye to success, don't let your modesty get in the way, don't be embarrassed to blow away some money on your team. Celebrating customer services successes makes your people feel valued, engenders a positive team spirit and, of course, reinforces the all important need to continuously strive towards the achievement of the customer service vision.

So take a step now to go and celebrate some of your team's customer service achievements over recent weeks.

Part 4

SOME CASE STUDIES

In this part of the book, a number of examples are given of organizations that have made tremendous strides in improving customer service, plus two anonymous examples of those that have failed rather poorly.

None of the organizations mentioned would claim to be perfect, and if it just so happens that you have had a bad experience with one of them recently, then I would beg your understanding and forgiveness.

The case studies do underline the key principles covered in the first three parts of this book.

SOME CASE STUDIES

[illegible]

[illegible]

[illegible]

39

British Airways

'We like passengers to feel, when they finish their journey on one of our aircraft, that we have gone that extra mile for them,' explains Val Gooding (British Airways Head of Cabin Services) 'that we have delivered that extra drink, that extra smile, that extra piece of information.'

HIGH LIFE, August 1991

The British Airways story is a classic.

In 1982, they were one of the so-called lame ducks of British industry, having announced a loss of £545 million. There had been major redundancies in the airline with staff numbers reducing from 59,000 in 1979 to a target of 35,000 by 1983. Their reputation among the travelling public was poor, their planes were often late, there were frequent industrial relations problems and generally passengers found British Airways staff, whilst professionally competent, cold, aloof, uncaring and bureaucratic.

By 1990, the airline had been turned around and was able to report record profits of £345 million. (In 1991, the profits dipped due to the Gulf War but rose to £285 million in 1992.)

Much of this success can be attributed to the implementation of two key visionary strategies, initiated and led by Sir Colin Marshall, Chief Executive, who was appointed in January 1983.

These visionary strategies focused on:

- An obsession with improving customer service;
- An obsession with improving British Airway's approach to management.

Experience with another airline, SAS, had shown that a passenger's rating of an airline depended on thousands of 'moments of truth'. The customer's perception, therefore, derived from a whole array of small experiences; for example, disinterested staff, smelly toilets, sloppy food, and so on. British Airways' research confirmed this, finding that a customer's view of the airline depended not solely on product, but their intuitive reaction to the ambience, environment and culture they experienced with the airline.

In their drive to achieve a greater number of positive 'moments of truth' for the customer, British Airways initiated a major training programme entitled 'Putting People First', which virtually everyone in the airline went through. It exposed airline employees to the new thinking about customer service, and stressed the critical role they had in contributing to this. Colin Marshall was so committed to this approach that he attended 97 per cent of the courses.

The courses were followed through with the establishment of Customer First Teams, whereby small groups were encouraged to contribute their ideas for improving customer service. Over 100 teams were set up and, of the thousands of ideas generated, over 700 were followed through and implemented.

British Airways recognized that customer care was, to a degree, a reflection of the care shown by its managers towards its employees. So, in addition to the 'Putting People First' programme, a six-day 'Managing People First' training course was introduced for all managers. Managers were shown how to coach, train and support their subordinates. Progress was measured in terms of how much they were prepared to delegate and whether the subordinate could be trusted to use judgement and discretion.

Managers were also trained to create a vision for the whole organization, so that they could identify with their top management group, followed by a vision for the group they managed.

Through this process, Colin Marshall began to dismantle much of the bureaucracy and hierarchy which constrained British Airways employees from exercising freedoms to care for the customer. It also helped change attitudes from cynical and defeatist to positive and friendly towards the customer.

Customer service continues to be a major component of the British Airways mission (see below) and provides an important focus for the efforts and energies of all staff.

It should be stressed that one of the reasons for British Airways' continuing success is that they 'keep at it'. The pursuit of the mission is ongoing. For them, customer service is not a passing fashion. Almost ten years after the introduction of 'Putting People First', British Airways are still concentrating their attention on improving customer service and on investing in their people by involving them in this process.

Thus in April 1992, British Airways launched yet another customer initiative, this time entitled 'Winning For Customers'. The programme is based on areas of concern and suggestions raised by the staff themselves following a company-wide staff input survey.

From April 1992 to October 1993, the airline's 48,000 employees, in groups of 140 a day, are being put through a carefully structured programme to press home the message that keeping customer loyalty is not only good news for travellers, but also makes sound business sense.

The 'Winning For Customers' programme follows a series of other initiatives since 'Putting People First', initiatives such as 'To Be the Best' and 'A Day in the Life'. British Airways are constantly initiating new and fresh approaches to help their staff improve customer service.

To quote Judy Robson, a senior executive with British Airways: 'We've learned that it is no use simply talking to people. You have to get them involved as much as possible . . . Furthermore,

THE BRITISH AIRWAYS MISSION

A company aiming

'TO BE THE BEST'

The corporate mission of British Airways is:

To be the best and most successful company in the airline industry.

The company's seven corporate goals are:

Safe and secure

To be a safe and secure airline

Financially strong

To deliver a strong and consistent financial performance

Global leader

To secure a leading share of air travel business worldwide with a significant presence in all major geographical markets

Service and value

To provide overall superior service and good value for money in every market segment in which we compete

Customer driven

To excel in anticipating and quickly responding to customer needs and competitor activity

Good employer

To sustain a working environment that attracts, retains and develops committed employees who share in the success of the company

Good neighbour

To be a good neighbour, concerned for the community and the environment all our people have to understand the whole service chain and exactly what role they play in it.'

What the customer has seen, as a result of British Airways' long-term pursuit of their mission, has been a whole range of improvements from better in-flight catering, to better facilities at airports, to warmer and friendlier staff. Furthermore, their flights now have a reputation for being punctual and their aeroplanes clean and pleasant to fly in.

What the shareholders have seen is a major improvement in profits.

The way the turn-round was achieved, was to focus on one critical goal – improving customer service – which every employee could relate and contribute to, and then focus on the way the company could manage to achieve this. Involvement of staff to secure their commitment has been a key aspect of the ongoing process and has meant substantial investments in training and development. In this way, British Airways have been able to translate a high-level vision, represented by a mere set of words, into a practical reality of a consistent pattern of positive experiences for their customers.

> **'Satisfaction from the job comes from feeling that, at the end of a flight, your passengers have had a good time and a good experience, and will want to fly again with BA. That is the biggest buzz I get.'**
>
> **Kirk Albrow, British Airways Purser.**
> **HIGH LIFE August 1991**

40

BMW Altwood of Maidenhead

A customer's perception:

'I think they are the best I have ever come across in terms of customer service. It is very easy to get through on the telephone and get your car booked in for service. Everyone is very polite.

'On arrival you are shown to a desk, there is rarely any waiting. You are treated as an individual. Coffee is available if you want it. They provide courtesy cars when your car is out of action. They also keep you constantly involved with the company – inviting you to various events to enjoy the "BMW" experience.

'On collecting my car from service, I always find it has been valeted and polished. Everything is over and above what you expect – and more than what you asked for.

'Summarily, they never let you down. I have no complaints at all.'

Director, major company

The General Manager, Alex Templer's explanation:

'We just believe that to be successful we have to excel at customer service. The concept is simple but very challenging. We spend a lot of time communicating the values relating to customer service and we are constantly striving to improve. We are always discussing customer service and spend a lot of time relearning what we know already.

'In practice, it means our customers have plenty of car parking outside the service reception area. It means we have a 24-hour reception facility. We try to create an ambience of cleanliness and spaciousness. Our workshops are spotless.

'We also give our front-line staff a lot of discretion. No longer do we have arguments between different departments as to whose budget it should come from when a customer comes in with a problem. We have a "coffer" account against which any employee can authorize expenditure to satisfy a customer in resolving a problem.

'We also aim to tell the truth. If a customer discovers a problem with a car which we hadn't discovered in the pre-sales check, and that leads to a bigger problem – then we tell the truth. We don't argue with the customer. We always admit our mistakes.

'There is a perception around that garages rip off their customers, provide poor service. We do everything to counteract that. We train all staff to be communicative with the customer, to explain what's going on, what the real problem is. We encourage them all to put themselves out for the customer.

'We see customer service as an art-form. There is no absolute. There are countless opportunities for doing better.

'After work, we frequently have ten minute debriefs with the receptionists, telephonists, invoicing people and workshop managers about what's been happening on the customer service front. Once a week, for an hour, the service manager will meet the team and talk through customer issues.

'We avoid queues like the plague. If a queue starts forming at reception, the Service Manager, the Workshop Manager and I will go down to serve the customers.

'We always rotate staff through different jobs – for example, reception, telephones and so on, to provide them with a variety of experience.

'We don't pare our resources to the bare minimum. For example, we hired a spare mechanic for peak workloads. He was over and above establishment. But we easily found work for him, even when there was no peak, and he has paid for himself many times over.

'Occasionally we have to get rid of people who don't do the job well. It's not too often. We have excellent mechanics and they complain if someone else is taking short-cuts. They take a pride in doing an excellent job. We train them from school and their performance is always under review. We aim to pay well and try to push pay up whenever we can.

'When things do go wrong, and occasionally they do, we use it as a learning experience. If I get a letter of complaint I get on the phone immediately.

'A lot of customer service is common sense. We try to hire people who will believe in our approach. We explain to people at interview what we want. We tell them that at Altwood we have a brand image based on integrity and honesty as well as professionalism. Everything we do must reflect that.

'I work on the long-term principle that to be successful we must develop people who believe in our approach and can put it into practice. I also believe in developing long-term relationships with our customers.

'I think we get it right because, as General Manager, I am really interested in our people and in them getting it right for our customers. We make people feel responsible for their decisions. The last thing we do is criticize our staff for making a mistake. What we do all the time is learn.'

41

A.N. Other car dealer

The following case is true, but the identities have not been revealed.

A customer's experience

'I bought my first car from this dealer just over two years ago when I saw the car in the showroom. It was a rather smart new executive car and the salesman, John Smith, was very successful in selling it to me. Everything since then, especially the after-sales service has been exceptionally poor. For example, it is incredibly difficult to get through to Service Reception to make an appointment for a service. Sometimes I've been kept hanging on the telephone for ten minutes. Out of frustration, I've rung the General Manager and he's made the appointment for me. This has happened on two or three occasions.

'Their car park for customers is always congested with breakdown vehicles and motorway wrecks. Sometimes it is impossible to park in the limited space they have available and you have to leave your car parked on the pavement in the busy road outside. To get to service reception you have to walk through a dark gloomy workshop with an oily floor and the sound of swearing mechanics and loud heavy metal music from the radio.

'They never seem to have enough people on reception and I always have to queue for a long time. Once, I nearly missed my train to London as a result, even though I had allowed fifteen minutes to check the car in. Amazingly, all around the wall are certificates proclaiming that various employees have been on customer service training courses.

'Last April, I went to collect my car from a service and found it wasn't ready. The car had 42,000 miles on the clock. So I decided to wander into the showroom to see what new cars they had available. There was one on show there, same model as my current one but with lots of additional features. They were offering it at an especially low price. I thought "This is the car for me!" There were three sales people in the showroom but none bothered to approach me.

'Finally, I went up to one of them and explained I was already a customer, had my existing car in for service and was interested in replacing it with this new one. The salesman asked me who had sold me the car last time. I told him "John Smith". To my amazement, he told me that John Smith wasn't around at present but if I'd care to call back tomorrow, John Smith would talk to me about this new car.

'I was flabbergasted. For a start, I wasn't planning to be around tomorrow and for all I knew, the car might have been sold by then. At my insistence this sales person attended to me. He wasn't really interested in selling to me, nor was he prepared to offer me much of a discount, nor did he attempt to sell me extras. I called down the General Manager (who I had met on previous occasions) and he attended to me. We made the deal.

'As I drove the new car away three days later, I discovered there was only 0.3 litre of petrol in the tank. On getting home, I also found that one of the headlight washers was missing. To be honest, all this made me very irate and yet once again I had to complain.

'On another occasion, after a service, I found a hub cap was missing. I mentioned this to the people on service reception. They said I must have lost it on the way to the service. I said that they had lost it. They didn't have a replacement in stock, I was told, but they would order one for me and let me know when it arrived. After four weeks, I had heard nothing. So I rang up. The hub cap had arrived, they told me, but they had mixed up the paperwork and were unable to contact me. My wife collected the hub cap (which they gave me free). When I went to fit it on Sunday afternoon, I found it was too small. It was the wrong hub cap. It took another week to get the problem fixed.

'I've had to move house since then. I notified them of my new address but they continue to mail me at my old address. What's worse, they have just mailed my old address asking me to return my old car (the one I sold back to them) for a battery cable safety check.

'I have discussed these problems with the General Manager on a number of occasions. He has always promised improvements but they never occur.'

42

AMI Healthcare

I went to meet Dr Marvin Goldberg, Chief Executive of AMI Healthcare, at their headquarters in Regent's Park. My appointment was at 4.00pm and I arrived at 3.45pm. The receptionist was very chatty and friendly.

At 3.50pm this gentleman wandered into reception and welcomed me. He was Dr Marvin Goldberg. He led me up two flights of stairs to his office, sat me down and offered me coffee which he poured himself.

I have met many Chief Executive in my time, but Dr Goldberg was the first one who had come downstairs personally to welcome me to his headquarters, let alone fetch coffee himself. Most Chief Executives send their secretaries to meet you at reception and then get them to arrange coffee.

I was duly impressed.

AMI Healthcare runs a number of hospitals around the country, including the Princess Margaret Hospital at Windsor, the Clementine Churchill Hospital at Harrow, and the Portland Hospital in central London.

Dr Goldberg explained to me that 'service' was the only thing that AMI Healthcare had to sell. They aimed to make that service friendly, welcoming and as comfortable as possible for their patients and customers. The company's overall ethos was that they were there for the patients.

It meant understanding their customers and, furthermore, understanding who their customers were. These were grouped into three categories:

1. Patients

As far as customer service was concerned, they aimed not only to give their patients the best medical care, but also the best non-medical care. This meant having an efficient and welcoming reception facility, friendly porters and helpful ancillary staff. It meant minimum bureaucracy (the last thing a traumatized patient entering a hospital wants is a lot of forms to fill in). It meant providing the maximum comfort for patients, together with the best possible facilities for them. It meant sustaining effective communications with patients at all times, especially in terms of keeping them informed of what was going on.

2. Patients' families

A key priority was to provide a sensitive and understanding service to patients' families. For example, AMI Healthcare ensured that families had easy telephone access to sisters and doctors regarding progress of relatives undergoing surgery or treatment. On visiting the hospital, patients' families would have access to first-class facilities with regard to waiting, meals and refreshments. Again, there would be excellent communications with sisters and doctors.

3. Doctors/consultants

AMI Healthcare saw doctors and consultants as their customers and wanted to ensure that they receive a really professional service when coming to an AMI Hospital to visit their patients, conduct clinics or undertake operations in theatre. This meant ensuring that doctors and consultants had ease of car parking, were recognized by receptionists and were able to work with teams of medical officers and nurses in whom the doctors and consultants had the greatest confidence. It also meant that all the information systems worked effectively (getting up-to-date case notes on patients to the consultant on time).

To achieve these high levels of customer service, Dr Goldberg explained, they started right at the beginning by hiring people who had the right sort of attitude towards the customer. They didn't recruit people who were indifferent to others.

They had developed within AMI Healthcare a management philsophy based on involving everyone in what was going on. It was a philosophy based on trust, integrity and valuing people. In terms of the latter, they had awards for employee of the month and year, as well as long service awards. They placed great store on effective communications. Dr Marvin Goldberg himself would regularly conduct 'fireside' chats with various groups of managers and staff to discuss what was going on. If there was a major piece of news or information which they wanted to communicate throughout the organization, they would aim to do this face-to-face for every single employee, within 24 hours.

They also aimed to be flexible by not having too many written rules. They wanted people to seize opportunities to please the customer and AMI would support them in doing so.

To achieve the highest standards, they had a quality assurance programme whereby each hospital was independently assessed once a year on the quality levels achieved. There were two types of assessment. In the first, the quality assurance team would look at the fabric of the hospital in terms of carpets, furniture, toilets, car parking, signage, catering, housekeeping and so on. In the second type, they would talk to patients and employees, as well as conduct a series of scheduled interviews with doctors and consultants. A quality assurance report would be written which would subsequently be reviewed by the board and the appropriate hospital director.

They believed in devolving management down to the lowest possible level. To that extent, each hospital director had a high degree of discretion on all aspects of running the hospital, as well as a fair degree of discretion on capital expenditure.

Training was also high priority and each hospital had a person accountable for training and development.

Finally, they believed that work should be fun. To this extent,

AMI Healthcare had initiated various social activities to achieve this, including picnics, Christmas parties, and birthday drinks for people.

43

Waterstone's Booksellers

The Waterstone's approach to bookselling and customer service is based on a number of simple principles. These include:

- Offering a wider range and a higher quality of stock than any other bookseller;
- A uniquely high level of staff knowledge and appreciation of books;
- A de-centralized structure placing discretion and responsibility with individual bookshop managers and staff.

The company is 'book' led and aspires to serve both the practical and emotional needs of its customers. A Waterstone's bookshop aims to be the epitome of what most people expect a bookshop to be. It is devoted to books – the book is a hero – a spirit of bookishness pervades every aspect of the company's operation.

In the view of Waterstone's, this philosophy of bookishness is totally consistent with the achievement of the more traditional goals of profitability and efficiency.

To apply these principles, Waterstone's have established four key goals which they call the 'Four Perfects':

1. Perfect Stock
2. Perfect Energy
3. Perfect Control
4. Perfect Service

Like other excellent customer service organizations, Waterstone's starts with the recruitment process, only hiring people who 'love' books and know about books. Waterstone's staff are trained in the art of bookselling and customer service. They are given a lot of accountability and discretion at an early stage. Whilst they have to hold certain core stocks (about 30 per cent of stock), store managers have total discretion over the balance of stock. This discretion can be and is delegated by store managers to their 'booksellers', who have accountability for stock in their sections. Each section will have approximately five categories of books (such as paperback fiction, humour etc.) The booksellers are people who can rapidly develop an excellent knowledge of the stock in their section and who feel totally at home with the product. These people have an 'innate feel' for books.

Many customers feel intimidated in a bookstore and are reluctant to ask for a book they can't find. Waterstone's staff will go out of their way to find a book for a customer when asked about a certain title.

Each store manager will have his or her own marketing budget and is encouraged to take initiatives to attract customers. Thus Waterstone's Hampstead stores holds a series of autumn evening events at which well-known writers will come and talk. Store managers also have their own training budget. A lot of the training will be informal and relate to stock as well as customer service. Managers are given regular management training, often using the facilities of Waterstone's parent company W H Smith.

Waterstone's also give their managers discretion on opening hours. Some stay open till 10.00pm whilst quite a few open on Sundays.

Teamwork is of the essence in any Waterstone's store, with managers providing a supportive role to their staff and ensuring they have clear standards to achieve. What the Directors look for when visiting a Waterstone's store is a manager who has:

1. An excellent feel for stock;
2. Developed an excellent front of shop;

3. Created the right atmosphere within the shop;
4. Achieved high morale amongst the staff.

All managers are appointed internally. The key career entry point is at bookseller level. From this, people can progress to senior bookseller and then on into management.

All staff have regular annual appraisals, when performance is assessed and targets set. For example one key target might be a customer compliments to complaints ratio of 2:1.

Branch managers report in to a small team of directors, who have a key task in establishing standards and ensuring that branch managers meet them. Directors regularly visit stores in their region to assess levels of service. In addition, every shop is annually subjected to a 'mystery shopper exercise', run by an outside consumer research company. Some examples of the criteria used in this exercise are:

1. Time taken to answer the phone
2. How the telephone was answered
3. Handling enquiries/book orders by telephone
4. Cleanness and attractiveness of window display
5. Window display content
6. Main message of window display
7. Location of display of opening hours
8. Number of customers in the shop
9. Location of window display books in store
10. Attitudes of staff
11. Number of staff available
12. Overall quality of response in making an enquiry about a book to a member of staff
13. Overall level of helpfulness of staff

14. Knowledge of staff
15. 'Salesmanship' (how hard the member of staff tried to sell a book)
16. Friendliness of staff
17. Enthusiasm of staff
18. Appearance of staff
19. Cleanliness and tidiness of store
20. Overall impression of store

The mystery shopper report provides data on how Waterstone's compares with other bookstores. The report, which is in detail, provides the basis for further improvements to customer service.

44

British Gas

British Gas is an organization that has progressively improved the service to its customers over many many years. The company measures its overall customer service with a rating on the scale:

- 167 Excellent
- 133 Very good
- 100 Good
- 83 Satisfactory
- 67 Fair
- 33 Poor
- 0 Very bad

When British Gas started measuring customer satisfaction almost 20 years ago, its rating was around the 80 mark. Its most recent score was over 120. Individual departments vary from around 110 through to 135.

Whether you read the Chairman's statements or the booklets available to its customers you will find a total commitment to service excellence.

British Gas's commitment to its customers was spelt out in a guide to the standards and quality of service it aims to give. The following is a summary of this commitment, made in April 1990:

British Gas's progressive improvement in customer service has been due to four main factors:

1. A long term approach to customer service (over 20 years working at it, no flash-in-the-pan once off gimmicky approaches);
2. A passionate commitment of the top team to customer service;

'During the year we conducted a survey among our 17 million domestic customers to find out how we performed against their criteria and expectations. I know of no other company which has undertaken such a survey on such a scale.

'We received 1.25 million replies. They showed us that, on the whole, whilst the great majority of customers are well satisfied, there were some areas of our work where we did less well than we did in others.

'Following the survey, we published a set of standards under the title "Commitment to our Customers". And that is exactly what it is. A commitment from us to deliver service excellence in all our dealings with customers.'

Extract from address to AGM
by Robert Evans, Chairman of British Gas
9 August 1990.

EXTRACT FROM BRITISH GAS'S ORIGINAL COMMITMENT TO CUSTOMERS

- **What you can expect when we meet or when we speak to you on the telephone or write to you**
- **How we will respond to your enquiries and requests for us to visit you**
- **What we will do if we are unable to keep an appointment with you**
- **How soon we can fit a cooker after you order it**
- **What happens if a repair requires a spare part**
- **How much notice we will give you if we need to get into your home for essential work**
- **What to do if you have problems**

3. A substantial investment in getting it right;
4. A positive attitude throughout the organization towards service.

British Gas sets out to listen to its customers. It surveys millions of them. The findings are used to develop customer sastisfaction ratings region by region and also to make the improvements customer require.

The successes in improving service are celebrated each year with the 'Gold Flame Awards' ceremony. Over a 1000 participants from around the country are transported to a venue in London (for example Alexandra Palace) where the award ceremony takes place. The ceremony is staged in a most professional and entertaining way and reinforces the company's overall commitment to customer service. The participants are treated to an excellent dinner the night before and a first-class lunch after the ceremony.

One key emphasis is on the 'behind the scenes' support people who make a major contribution to service. These 'unsung heroes and heroines' are included in the Gold Flame Award process.

British Gas believes in investing in improving service, not only through expensive celebrations, but also in the way it communicates with its customers and in developing the systems required to satisfy its customers. There is also a substantial investment in training.

A major re-organization has taken place with the sole aim of providing a fully integrated service to the customer. ('We don't want the customer to see the joins in our organization.') This means that every employee is encouraged to think British Gas, as opposed to confining their thinking to service engineering, or showrooms, or accounts, or distribution. Their aim is to eliminate the 'them and us' attitude found in many other organizations, which is typified by 'It's not my problem, love, you'd better ring the people in accounts'.

Service engineers are encouraged to communicate with customers if perchance they are stuck in a motorway traffic jam and can't get to the job on time. They are encouraged to leave the premises they have been working on as clean and tidy as possible – as if it were their own home. After each job, an 'impression card' is left for the customer to make any comments. These cards are carefully studied and a number of improvements have been made as a result (for example, in relation to the appointments system).

Until recently, there had been a steady reduction in the number of complaints as a result of British Gas's long-term drive to improve customer service. Paradoxically, following recent initiatives to encourage customers to provide feedback, together with the introduction of a new complaints handling procedure, the number of complaints has increased.

The front-line people are given a lot of freedom to please the customer. For example, if the customer's central heating needs a spare part, the engineer will do everything possible to get that part to the customer. The paperwork catches up later. Service engineers have an important role to play in deciding what spares they carry in their vans.

Local initiative is encouraged, as are ways of being of practical help to customers. For example, if a customer urgently needs a new cooker which is not available from the appliance warehouse, it can be removed from the showroom display and delivered to the customer on the day of the purchase.

A series of training workshops have been run on customer relations – looking at issues like telephone handling, calling customers by their name, the importance of saying 'thank you' and so on. The overall purpose of the workshops is to encourage British Gas employees to show that they really care for their customers and are both friendly and professional.

From a management point of view, it means continually striving for excellence. Each year, British Gas managers set themselves tougher and tougher targets. British Gas employees have immense pride in their work and a high degree of belief in the products they sell and the services they provide. The role of manager is seen as sustaining this pride and belief. The company rewards its people both financially and non-financially for excellent performance.

It has all meant a massive culture change involving restructuring, developing an open and honest style of communications – not only with British Gas's employees, but also customers and the media.

In British Gas's view, their customers are demanding even higher standards. This means setting clear goals, clear standards and clear values. It means helping employees reach their full potential, it means encouraging innovation and responding positively to change. It means teamwork throughout, at the top, as well as at the frontline. It means involvement. For example the 'Commitment to Customers' was discussed with all regions to determine that they could live with all the standards set in it.

In April 1992, British Gas re-launched their 'Commitment to Customers' and this was accompanied by the announcement of Standards of Service which have planned performance levels and an undertaking to publish actual performance levels each year; a fixed payment of compensation when certain standards are not achieved; and a visible complaint handling procedure, which will take a customer directly to the local District Manager.

At the 1992 AGM held on 30 April, Robert Evans, the Chairman of British Gas, said 'Last month we announced a new Commitment to Customers which includes cash compensation payments if we let our customers down. I don't expect us to have to pay out much compensation. This is not an investment in failure. It is an investment in doing things right first time. It requires a new way of thinking – a new culture throughout the Company.'

45

East Dorset District Council

In 1989, East Dorset District Council won the Tom Peter's 90-day excellence challenge for local government authorities in the South. The criteria the judges based their assessment on were:

- tangible improvements to customer service;
- involvement at all levels of the organization;
- engendering the attitude that 1,000 things can be improved by 1 per cent as opposed to one thing being improved by 100 per cent;
- the sincerity of the objectives;
- the degree to which initiatives can be sustained beyond the 90-day challenge;
- the level of innovation and creativity achieved in improving customer service.

East Dorset is a small district authority with around 300 employees serving a population of 80,000. In summer 1987, a new Chief Executive, Alan Breakwell, was appointed. One of the first things he did was to take his new team away for three days to reflect where the authority was going, what were its key objectives, what role the Chief Officers and the rest of the staff had to play and to determine exactly who were their customers. As a group, they decided to improve customer care, place a greater emphasis on training, as well as recruiting and retaining the best employees. They also decided to move forward on information technology.

During 1988, a number of working parties were set up to involve as many people as possible in the achievement of these objectives. One of the important things that evolved was a set of key values for the council. These eventually emerged in a document 'Statement of Management Priorities', published in July 1989 (see below).

EXTRACT FROM: EAST DORSET DISTRICT COUNCIL'S STATEMENT OF MANAGEMENT PRIORITIES, JULY 1989

KEY VALUES: EXCELLENCE through:
Respect for the individual employee; Caring for the customers; Competitiveness; Adaptability to change

CARING FOR CUSTOMERS: AIMS:
Ensure that the council knows its customers.
Dedicate sufficient resources to service customers well.
Helpful attitude at point of contact.
Improve quality of service delivery.
Assess customer satisfaction.

ACTION REQUIRED

a) **Adopt a consumer approach to Council services and ensure effective complaints procedures (*Department Groups with coordination by Working Party*)**
b) **Review how services are made available to the public and consider improvements (*Department Groups with coordination by Working Party*)**
c) **Dedicate adequate space and resources to customer reception areas (*Chief Officers*)**
d) **Consider a Council presence outside Furzehill and become more active in going out to meet customers (*Chief Officers and Members*)**
e) **Customer care training programme for all employees (*Training Group*)**
f) **Action programme for responding to telephone calls and acknowledging letters (*Training Group*)**

Half-day training sessions were run for everyone, using in-house trainers. During the sessions, staff were encouraged to think of ideas they could implement, and to identify problems. At each session, there was voting for the best overall ideas package and prizes were awarded. The training sessions generated more ideas than could have been imagined in the first place, together with an immense amount of enthusiasm and a will to succeed. Most importantly, the staff wanted action.

The working party and training group worked to turn these ideas into action and staff were kept informed by newsletters, posters, and briefings. There was also an 'ideas into action' barometer in reception. Chief Officers were kept informed through department working groups. The customers were also told what was happening.

Over 1000 ideas were generated of which about 25 per cent were really original. Some of these ideas are listed below:

- Late night opening one day a week;
- The Chief Executive to carry out reception duties once a week;
- Name badges for staff with colour codes for different departments;
- A visitors' book in main reception with space for comments;
- Toys and games in reception for children waiting with parents;
- Coffee machines available in reception;
- More car parking space for visitors;
- A survey asking customers what they thought of East Dorset District Council;
- A quick response to complaints (with Chief Officers responsible for seeing all complaints for their departments);
- An open day for customers;
- A hand-book for customers.

The overall lessons learned by East Dorset were that to be successful they had to have total commitment at the top, a lot of teamwork, and everyone had to be working towards the same objective. Furthermore, it was important to have to take risks in making improvements – not just to sit there and talk about it. Another key lesson was that they involved everyone. To miss out one single person would have created difficulties. Involving staff helped them determine what was really expected of them and enabled them to give a very positive response.

Overall, it engendered a spirit of pride in the successes achieved.

The customer care programme is ongoing with departmental service days, further working parties looking at communications and customer care, regular team briefings, various customer surveys and new initiatives such as task forces on litter.

To win the Tom Peters' award, a team from the customer service working group, including a junior secretary, the trees officers, the chief executive, the chairman and, most importantly, a customer, presented to the judges the successes the council had achieved during the 90-day period.

What was achieved overall, was a change of attitude by council staff towards its customers. The simple message was that the public are their customers and that there are always going to be 1000 opportunities to improve the service to them.

46

Bank of Scotland

The Bank of Scotland's approach to its customers is based on a number of key strategic aims. These focus on professionalism, consistency, innovation and excellent customer relations.

The accent on professionalism permeates the whole organization. Bank of Scotland people know what they are talking about, know what they are doing and work to the highest standards. They get things done. To quote one Director: 'It's sheer bloody professionalism that differentiates us from other banks'. In fact, in 1989, a survey in the Economist resulted in the Bank of Scotland being voted 'The most admired bank', by its banking peer group.

Professionalism also means responding quickly and effectively to customer needs. Thus on the residential mortgages side, Bank of Scotland Central Banking Services issues a 'Declaration of Service' to their customers (see next page).

The Bank of Scotland aims to retain the long respected banking virtues of conservatism, consistency and solidity. This has been characterized in many ways, for example, in 1987, it decided not to pay high but fashionable prices to enter the capital markets business. It has meant a continuing determination to keep its ratio of operating expenses at a lower level than any other UK clearing bank. It has meant resisting the development of an expensive branch network in England. Such 'solidity' benefits the customer. It is a bank that does not take high risks.

Consistency is coupled with professionalism in that the Bank of Scotland wants its customers to feel it can always be relied upon to provide fast, effective and friendly service. Trust and integrity are key components in achieving such consistency.

BANK OF SCOTLAND
C.B.S. - RESIDENTIAL MORTGAGES
DECLARATION OF SERVICE

1. **All completed mortgage applications will be given a decision, in principle within 48 hours of receipt.**
2. **All correspondence will be replied to within 24 hours of receipt.**
3. **All incoming telephone calls will be answered within three rings.**
4. **If unable to be resolved immediately, all telephone enquiries will be responded to within 24 hours.**
5. **All requests for additional borrowing will be referred to the original introducer in order that the appropriate life cover may be arranged.**
6. **All mortgage customers will be contacted by letter on an annual basis with details of additional mortgage related services which are available.**

Balanced against the need to be consistent, is the need to innovate. One of the services that the Bank of Scotland has pioneered is its electronic Home and Office Banking Services (HOBS), enabling customers to carry out their banking from their home or office. The attraction to customers is that HOBS is available all hours, including weekends, that there are no queues, that statements can be produced on the screen on demand. It enables customers to settle their bills electronically, check standing orders and direct debits and, basically, carry out all the routine banking transactions. As a customer, you can instruct the system to make payments on any date you want, thus saving the interest cost of making payments too early.

Back in 1983, the Bank of Scotland was the first UK clearing bank to introduce a high interest cheque account as a service to its customers. This innovation was subsequently copied by most other banks.

Developing excellent relationships with customers is also high priority for the Bank of Scotland. Personalized letters and personal contact are given great emphasis. Managers aim to get out and about, to know their customers, to really understand their problems and (if corporate customers) know how their companies work. The overall aim is to treat customers like human beings, rather than a series of account numbers.

To achieve high levels of service, the Bank of Scotland has continually worked at developing its approach to management. Teamwork is the key. 'Moulded' teams of accountants, lawyers and bankers work closely together to provide the required service.

There is a significant investment in training at all levels, during which the importance of customer service is continually stressed and reinforced.

The top team works very closely together and, overall, a high degree of trust and understanding is developed throughout the organization. Lines of communication are short, with a relatively flat structure (which means that the Bank of Scotland has between a quarter and a third of the management overhead of some of its competitors).

Short lines of communication facilitate a quick, effective response to customers and a higher quality of decision making. As a result, there is a lot of enthusiasm everywhere for doing business, work is seen to be fun. People throughout the Bank of Scotland care about customer service because they know directly that the senior team really cares too.

Perhaps that's why the Bank of Scotland's slogan is 'A friend for life'.

47

Cornhill Insurance

Most customers come into contact with insurance companies when they have major problems. Often, insurance companies exacerbate the problem with excessive bureaucracy and by creating difficulties in meeting claims and making payments which are sometimes delayed for months. Overall, the industry has a bad reputation for its lack of sensitivity towards its customers who, more often than not, are suffering the trauma of great losses.

Cornhill Insurance aims to achieve the reverse. It aims to be part of the solution to the customer's problem rather than part of the problem. Its dominant theme is that 'Cornhill Cares'.

On 25 January 1990, Britain suffered a major storm which inflicted a lot of damage, around the country. Cornhill Insurance received an additional 17,500 claims over and above its normal workload. The majority of these descended upon the company's claims department, in a short space of time. The handling of these claims was further complicated by the exceptional winter weather that prevailed for the following four to five weeks. The repair of property was mainly in the hands of external tradespeople but, where necessary, Cornhill staff did give advice, such as where this expertise could be found. None of the customers was kept waiting for advice. There was no delay in authorizing repairs, and wherever 'money' was the answer to the problem, this was immediately forthcoming. This was achieved by the claims staff working long hours, and staff from other Cornhill branches, who were less affected by the storms, willingly agreeing to be temporarily transferred into the worst hit areas, in order to assist their colleagues.

Another example of putting their 'Cornhill Cares' approach into practice is the provision of a twenty-four hours a day, seven days per week service – which is frequently used – for customers with travel policies, who experience a medical emergency abroad. Within one hour of telephoning a UK number, the customer will be talking to a member of staff who will provide practical help. This could range from giving advice or reassurance that medical bills will be paid, to guaranteeing to a local hospital that Cornhill will pay their charges, or to finding seats on aircraft to bring home the 'walking wounded', or arranging repatriation of the seriously injured by air ambulance.

Another general area where 'Cornhill Cares' is a countrywide organization of Approved Repairers and Damage Assessment Centres, at strategic locations. These minimize the paperwork following a road accident and speed up the authorization of repairs and the return of the vehicle to the road.

Specific cases of 'Cornhill Cares' are given below.

Overall, Cornhill Insurance seeks to add value to the basic insurance cover by providing advice, assistance and a service, which treats their customers like individuals.

It goes out of its way to ensure that customers have every facility to overcome their problems. For example, customers with car insurance policies will have a 'Motorcall' card to carry in their wallets. This card contains the policy number, together with helpline numbers for accidents, legal help and windscreen replacements. Householders are provided with a 'Homecall', twenty-four hour emergency service.

. . . A policyholder suffered a road accident in France. On conclusion of his claim he wrote 'I would like to add that when the accident happened we received tremendously good service from the lady we dealt with at Cornhill Insurance European Claims Department. She could not have been more helpful and what to us was a calamity was sorted out in the most efficient and capable manner possible. We cannot praise her too highly.'

. . . A policy holder purchased a new car. He drove it home and parked it in his garage. The petrol tank was full. There was a fault on his central heating boiler which was situated in his garage. A fire ensued and engulfed his new car which exploded, rendering it a total loss. The policyholder reported the claim on the day of the accident and the car was inspected by Cornhill's engineer on the same day. On the following day a new car was delivered to the policyholder.

. . . A policyholder was involved in an accident on his way to work. His vehicle was damaged, but mobile. He telephoned Cornhill's local office who advised him to take his car to a Damage Assessment Centre. This he did, and his car was inspected at 9.30am. Because the repair was only small, Cornhill's engineer telephoned an Approved Repairer who collected the car within ten minutes and took the policyholder to work. The repair was completed the same day and the car delivered to the policyholder's office.

'Cornhill's objective is to expand its business in a profitable and dependable manner, by concentrating on meeting customers' needs for security.

'This will be achieved by building relationships, not simply by issuing paper products. This requires the development of a service culture at every level, which delivers and demonstrates care and concern for customers, intermediaries and staff.

'Everyone has a part to play in making this a success. Every point of contact with our customers and intermediaries, in person, by telephone or in writing; with underwriters, with the claims department, with the sales force, with the accounts department, or indeed any other department, either helps to build a proper relationship or puts that relationship and that customer at risk.

'These essential ideas can be simply expressed:

"Cornhill Cares".'

Statement from Ray Treen, General Manager, 2 January 1990

The achievement of high standards of customer care derives from the mission established by the top team for the 1990s (see previous page).

To achieve this mission, all Cornhill staff participated in a series of workshops that were run in 1990. Each workshop contained people from different departments. Hundreds of ideas were generated, many of which the company was able to follow through. In addition, there were a series of management workshops at branch and department level.

Feedback from all these workshops was provided to senior managers. The key was to get ownership of the 'caring' approach, and to avoid 'wish-lists' of things staff wanted senior management to do.

The big test for Cornhill will be in a series of customer satisfaction surveys.

Overall, Cornhill sees its quest for improving customer care as one that will extend right through the 1990s. No matter how good the company is today, it sees that there will always be opportunities for improvement tomorrow.

48

ICL

Over the last ten years, ICL has turned itself around from being one of the consistent lame ducks of British industry, to an incredibly successful computer company that is outstripping its competitors by many measures of company performance. For example, its return on capital employed is higher than most of its competitors. Also, its record, over the years, on improving profit before tax is far better than most others.

Much of this can be attributed to ICL's visionary approach to developing its business. To succeed in the 1990s the company is focusing on three key strategic directions:

1. Success by supplying specialist IT and industry expertise and using Open Systems standards as the framework for the solutions provided by ICL;
2. Directing the company's investments at specific markets to deliver services, solutions and local applications needs. (For example ICL has, over recent years, concentrated on developing and delivering systems for the retail market);
3. Developing collaborations with third parties to provide the best components, products and access to markets.

This visionary strategy is built on partnerships with clients, suppliers and associates. ICL sees quality as fundamental to the way in which it carries out its business. This is reflected in their drive for excellence in industry markets and professional expertise. To achieve these visionary aims, the company has developed the '*ICL WAY . . . "the way we do things around here . . ."* '

The ICL WAY is based on seven key commitments:

1. Commitment to Change;
2. Commitment to Customers;
3. Commitment to Excellence;
4. Commitment to Team-Work;
5. Commitment to Achievement;
6. Commitment to People Development;
7. Commitment to Creating a Productivity Showcase.

ICL sees its managers as being accountable for translating into practice the attitudes expressed in the seven commitments. Each manager has ten obligations which are an integral part of their job. These obligations are:

1. Business manager: people manager;
2. Direction;
3. Strategic thinking;
4. High-value outputs;
5. Teamwork;
6. Development of people;
7. 'Can-do' attitude;
8. Innovation;
9. Difficult issues (facing up to them);
10. Self measurement.

ICL has an extensive and ongoing management education programme to help managers meet their obligations, honour their commitments to customers and employees alike, and contribute to the achievement of the long-term visionary strategy of the company. Attendance at these 'core' programmes starts with the board. One of the overall purposes is to develop a shared set of values, together with a clear understanding of strategic objectives.

Customer service in ICL is viewed from two different levels:

1. Material service (systems reliability, delivery times etc.)
2. Personal service (attitudes of employees)

There is an ongoing process of competitive benchmarking on customer satisfaction to measure success at each of these levels.

There are constant attempts to improve service to customers. For example, to provide a more effective response to callouts, a centralized call reception centre has been established for the whole country. A high-tech centre with state of the art techniques, it concentrates on resolving problems customers encounter. It includes a diagnostic support unit for getting to the root cause of the problem. As soon as a customer rings through to the call reception centre, requesting help to resolve a problem (hardware or software), there is a commitment to have an expert call back within twenty minutes, to talk through the problem and decide the appropriate course of action.

Telephone response times are monitored against the following targets:

97% of calls answered within 10 seconds
98% of calls answered within 20 seconds
99% of calls answered within 30 seconds
99.6% of calls answered before customer rings off

In practice, the average answer time is two seconds. 'Telephone talk time' is regularly monitored to promote efficiency. Customers who ring the call reception centre are led through a structured dialogue to help focus on the problem. The average talk time is two minutes.

Other targets are set on service support. For example the number of repeat calls is targeted at 5 per cent (the number of call-backs to fix the same problem). Arrival times versus the estimated time communicated to the customer is also monitored.

If any branch is not on target, the situation is reviewed and corrective action initiated.

Overall, there is a target of five hours to fix a problem, this is the time lapsing between the original call and the point at which the engineer walks away, having resolved the problem. The average time achieved, in fact, is four and a half hours. Every engineer will deposit a prepaid reply card after a visit, asking the customer for comments on the service. These are sent to branch managers.

Customers are regularly surveyed on their satisfaction with ICL using an overall rating along the scale of:

1	=	Very dissatisfied
5	=	Somewhat dissatisfied
6	=	Somewhat satisfied
10	=	Very satisfied

There is also a major 'ICL's image in Britain' survey of major companies (including many who are not customers) in Great Britain. The survey includes interviews with Directors. From this survey, the top six issues that ICL needs to address, in terms of image, are identified.

Managers are accountable for undertaking 'care visits' to customers. Each has a target number of care visits, which are proactively arranged in advance with each customer. Reports are logged for each visit.

ICL uses a wide range of other customer service measures in addition to the ones mentioned above.

There is a lot of recognition activity by ICL, in relation to customer service achievements, for example a programme of gold and silver awards for customer service. To reinforce the commitment to customers, ICL has an 'investing in people' programme, consisting of various training and development activities. Improving quality is also a major feature of the company's development programmes, with line managers playing a major role in training their staff to seek ways of improving quality. They are taught to appreciate the high cost of non-conformance when it comes to quality. Quality improvement brainstorms are carried out with the 'top ten' improvement ideas being identified at every level (from the UK as a whole, to each division). Everything possible relating to customer service and quality is monitored, from the performance of the switchboard to the way complaints are handled, from telephone handling to the image of the sales force.

All managers and staff throughout the organization are involved in setting specific customer care and quality objectives which they have to achieve.

Employees are regularly surveyed for their opinions about a wide range of things in the company (for example, on communications and on the support they get from their managers).

Overall, ICL's success stems from a very clear sense of direction, a clear sense of commitment to its customers and employees, and a substantial investment in helping its managers and employees achieve these visionary objectives.

49

H+C

H+C (Hammond and Champness) is a major European company which manufactures, services and repairs lifts. You will see their attractive, glass-caged lifts at the Science Museum in London, at the Putney Exchange shopping mall, or in the atrium of the impressive modern offices of the London Borough of Richmond at Twickenham.

In 1990, Eric Jones, Director of Service and Repair, worked with his Regional Managers to develop a major 'Customer Initiative', to improve service levels across the company. This was backed up with a major investment in training, entitled 'The Training Challenge'. The latter was video-based and aimed to help H+C's skilled lift engineers further develop their professional capabilities in modern lift technology.

One of the first things Eric Jones and his Managing Director, Nigel Davis, did was take their colleagues on the Board away for two days to develop a long term strategy for moving forward on the 'Customer Initiative'. Staying at a remote farmhouse location in the Cotswolds – and employing a consultant as a facilitator, the Directors focused their attention on what they really wanted to achieve through the 'Customer Initiative' and how they would get there.

They decided that there were six critical standards of customer service which they had to get right to be successful during the 1990s.

These were:

- Safety
- Responsiveness
- Dependability

- Communication
- Appearance
- Commitment

The Directors also reviewed their approach to management. It was already highly decentralized, and they agreed that this was a strength they would need to build upon. Each of the thirty or so Branch Managers across the UK had a high degree of autonomy in terms of achieving their year end profit targets. What was critical, was encouraging each Branch Manager to take the 'Customer Initiative' forward at local level.

A series of two-day training workshops were set up, initially for Regional Managers and then for Branch Managers. These were held at various locations throughout the UK. The same consultant who had worked with the Board was used. The purpose of these workshops was to stimulate managers into thinking what they would do personally to further progress the 'Customer Initiative'. The consultant then met with each group for one day on a regular six-monthly basis to review progress and further develop ideas about the 'Customer Initiative' and the steps that should be taken.

Within eighteen months, a large number of achievements had been reported (see below).

Part of the initiative was to get closer to the customer, to determine what he or she felt about the service provided by H+C. A number of open days were held around the country, together with a regular customer survey and the establishment of customer panels.

Measuring the overall success of the 'Customer Initiative' initially appeared a little more difficult. Traditionally, the company's main focus had been on profitability and other financial parameters. Inevitably, this led to a risk of 'short-term' thinking and the sacrifice of longer-term strategies (such as the 'Customer Initiative') which did not show any immediate financial return.

The Board therefore decided to develop its approach to Performance Management to include a number of critical non-financial 'Customer Initiative' performance parameters (see below).

H+C THE CUSTOMER INITIATIVE

SOME TANGIBLE ACHIEVEMENTS

- Safety
  - Video training modules (The Training Challenge)
  - Site safety assessment
  - Issue of alarm devices
  - Issues of Chief Engineer's instructions
  - Issue of 'Safety Lines' (newsletter)
  - Safety training programme
  - Safety committee
  - Sub-contractors working policy
  - Safety policy statement
- Responsiveness
  - Telephone answering manner
  - Quicker response times
  - Improved technical support
  - Standards for internal systems improved
- Dependability
  - Quality Control by Engineering Department
  - Service guides
  - BS 5750 accreditation
- Communication
  - Regular meetings held at ALL levels
  - New internal publications for 2-way communication
  - Closer to customers all round
  - Customer newsletter issued
  - Open days
  - Hi-Lines (product information for Field Staff)
- Appearance
  - New logos on vans/overalls
  - New overalls/uniforms
  - New office signs
  - I.D. badges
  - Service and Repair Division ties
  - Paper mats to protect carpets
  - Vacuum cleaners for lift engineers
- Commitment
  - Ongoing training programmes
  - Product development
  - Ongoing safety training for ALL
  - Engineers' calling cards

H+C 'CUSTOMER INITIATIVE'

NON-FINANCIAL PERFORMANCE PARAMETERS

- Safety
  - Number of reported accidents
- Responsiveness
  - Average response time
  - Average down time
- Dependability
  - Service visits actual/scheduled × 100
  - Repeat calls per lift on service
- Communication
  - No. of written complaints
  - No. of written compliments
- Appearance
  - Performance check-list
  - Have standards been achieved
- Commitment
  - Majors: No. of late completions
    No. of early completions
  - Minors: No. of jobs 〉 2 months old
  - Lifts on service : Start of month
    End of month

These non-financial performance parameters are now being applied to Regional Directors and will gradually extend all the way down the line to front-line engineers.

With the development of the 'Training Challenge' on the engineering side, the Board felt it important to review career structures, for its engineers to ensure that the competencies they were developing were duly accredited and rewarded. The Board decided to move towards establishing a high status, highly qualified 'Customer Service Engineer' who would no longer be on an hourly rate. This person would not only have developed a high level of competency in lift engineering and technology, but also in customer service and business appreciation.

Within the first eighteen months, the overall investment in the 'Customer Initiative' exceeded half-a-million pounds. Whilst it is difficult to relate this investment directly to profitability – the company is showing an increasing market share, an increasing awareness of and interest in the 'Customer Initiative' by customers – and most importantly – increasing levels of revenue and profit.

50

Crying all the way to the bank

Article by Miles Kington in The Independent *newspaper, 18 December 1990*
(Reprinted with permission)

Recently, my bank sent me a form to fill in. They hoped that if I answered all the questions correctly (How often do you use your branch a week? What services do you ask for most often? Can you ever hear anything the cashier says back to you? etc.), they would be able to make their bank's performance even more perfect than before.

However, as I ran my eye down the form I realized that it would take me a long time to fill it in accurately, that I didn't have that sort of time to spare and that I had no real confidence that, even if filled in, the form would benefit me personally. In other words, it would be like queueing in the very same bank all over again.

So, in the space reserved for any other comments, I wrote: 'If it had not been for the large overdraft which I had till very recently, I would have moved banks many years ago. For nearly 30 years I have been a customer of yours, and in all that time I can honestly say I have never encountered a more inefficient, time-wasting and badly organized business set-up. I will gladly supply details on request.'

That was two months ago. They have not been back to ask for

details, which suggests that either they are not totally sincere in wanting to improve their service, or they really are inefficient. I am sorry about this, as I feel I could help them more than most.

What I said was perfectly true, although I didn't spell out the fact that if you have an overdraft, it is better to be with an inefficient bank than a red-hot one. Over the years, I have known some very nice people at my bank, and on a personal level it has always worked well; it's just that when it comes to paperwork, the bank seems incapable of sending the form I need, the statement I want, or of getting the simplest thing right over the phone. And they still can't work out a system of queueing or devise a window through which you can be heard without shouting. I suppose I am asking a lot.

Mind you, they are not without initiative. I remember once being fairly desperate for a new cheque book and sending a request to my home branch for one. It never came. I finally rang up and demanded to know why.

'Oh, yes, Mr Kington, we got the request, but the signature looked a bit different from usual so we decided to ignore it.' Not decided to check back with you or anything, just decided to ignore it. That was years ago. Less than a month ago, I went to my bank to get some travellers' cheques, which need to be ordered two or three days in advance. I stood at the window for 10 minutes waiting for someone to come. Nobody came, so I went to the bank next door and got my travellers' cheques over the counter – not within two days, but in two minutes.

I got into this bank for the simple, though not good, reason that my father had always banked there, and my son recently revealed that he, too, had drifted into banking with them.

'Have they always been this inefficient, Dad,' he asked, 'or am I just unlucky?'

'Good heavens, what on earth can you mean?'

'Well, quite apart from always sending me the wrong form, they have a very unfortunate phone technique. Whenever I ring up the bank, the bloke at the other end is always in the middle of telling his colleagues a story. He asks me to hold on so that he can finish the story. He then puts his hand over the phone – they can't even afford a proper cut-off device – and goes on with his story, but half the time he doesn't cover it very well and I can hear the story.'

'And you're complaining that . . .'

'Yes. They're terrible stories.'

My son has also identified a knowledge gap in his bank. The gap is between the man at the window, who doesn't know the answer to my son's question, and the chap at the desk at the back, who does know the answer, but refuses to come to the window because it's beneath his dignity. This leads to a to-and-froing between the customer and the man at the back, with cashier as go-between – which can take the best part of an afternoon.

'Honestly, Dad, I don't know how you stuck with them for so long.'

'Well, I suppose I'm afraid deep down that all banks might be exactly the same.'

'Are you sure it wasn't to get an article out of it all one day?'

Perhaps it was. Yes, perhaps it was.

51

The American experience

It was over five years since I had been to America and I thought I would return – as a simple customer – to experience a small sample of the service there and to compare it with Europe. After all it was the Americans who coined the phrase 'customer service' as a modern management concept, and it was the Americans who always seemed to be acclaimed for their superb service, or so the delegates on my Customer Service Workshops were always telling me.

I was not disappointed. The first impression on arriving at Orlando Airport was one of spaciousness, cleanliness and modernity. Everything seemed to be working and of high quality. The immigration official was very friendly and even chatted to the children, and the luggage conveyor belts were of gleaming metal rather than the dilapidated scratched rubber you see in Britain. There was even someone to line the luggage up on the belt to prevent it jamming.

The Lindo-Dollar car rental collection arrangements were equally impressive, with an efficiency rarely found in Britain. There were no long waits for the bus to take you to the off-airport car rental depot. At the check-in, there was no queueing and the people there were very friendly and prepared to spend as long as you liked talking you through the car rental agreement, as well as go to some lengths to explain the best route to your destination.

Having checked in, a young man in uniform introduced himself to me, 'Hi, I'm Antoine, I'll be collecting your car for you – if you'd like to wait right here, I'll be back with your car in two minutes.'

And he was, helping me load our cases into the car's boot (or should I say trunk?).

Our flight from Gatwick had been delayed four hours because of fog and it was 11.00pm before we arrived at our rental villa at Kissimmee. We were all dehydrated and there was no food of any type in the villa. Being America, this posed no problem, we simply went to the Kash 'n' Karry supermarket nearby – a large, bright, clean store with plenty of fresh produce. Like many supermarkets, it is open 24 hours a day, 364 days a year. So we shopped at midnight (and we weren't the only customers). Kash 'n' Karry, which we subsequently used many times, have a policy that if there are more than three customers queueing, then they will open another till – and they do. The same thing even happened at the US Post Office where more tills opened when a queue formed.

Most people do actually want to serve you in America, they do want to put themselves out for you. In quite a few of the restaurants, the more you demanded of the waiters and waitresses the happier they seemed to be. 'More coffee sir? No problem!' They actually take a delight in explaining the menu to you and explaining the procedures.

Another day, I went to the Barnett Bank of Florida to change some travellers cheques. The lady who served me leant over the counter and started chatting to my five-year-old daughter, before offering her the choice of a lollipop or cookie. Would that happen in Britain?

Having seen the Tom Peter's video extolling the virtues of Walt Disney World, we decided to check it out. Again we were suitably impressed. Everything is immaculately clean and everything works (unlike in Britain where I frequently struggle with hotels to get an Overhead Projector that works). Whilst you cannot escape the queues at Walt Disney World, or at the phenomenal Epcot Centre – they have at least devised procedures which keep the queues moving and entertain you at the same time. Even so, there were certain aspects of the service which grated, for example an obsession with safety (or avoidance of litigation I suspect) such that we were constantly told to use handrails, to step carefully off the moving walkway, to stand clear of doors about to open. Even on the old-fashioned, double-decker buses safety ropes are carefully placed across the platform, just in case someone attempts to fall off as the bus travels at five miles per hour. And of course standing on a moving bus is strictly forbidden!

Despite all the emphasis on service – certain things seem to be missing, especially in many American restaurants, where the prime function focuses on the quick, efficient provision and consumption of value-for-money food. The concepts of cuisine, ambience and conviviality are rarely to be found. The highways are cluttered with signs proclaiming 'All you can eat breakfast $1.99', 'All you can eat steak and shrimps $7.99', 'Salad bar – make as many trips as you like.' Pizzas are guaranteed within five minutes of ordering – or the next one is free.

Value for money is everything – one waitress at Black Angus Restaurant seemed quite surprised we had not brought any discount vouchers with us. You don't even have to think about the tip you give in some places – at the bottom of the bill the 'recommended tip' is explicitly stated. 'Are you happy if I add the recommended tip of $6 to your credit card voucher sir?'

In America, they continually try to innovate when it comes to customer service. Here are some examples:

- Games of solitaire on restaurant tables
  (*International House of Pancakes*)
- Free coffee at the store entrance
  (*Waldenbooks*)
- Computer-printed schedules at tourist attractions – you arrive at 11.00am and on the map provided is printed a list of suggested times (starting 11.30am) to visit each attraction and show
  (*Sea World*)

- The waiter doesn't wait to be asked to bring extra napkins, he sees that you need more and brings them
(*Gilligans restaurant*)
- Stamps by mail – delivered within 3 days, no service charge
(*US Post Office*)
- Pen Pal Club
(*US Post Office*)
- Free 'Clean-up' service on your mailing list – submit the addresses and the computer will check and correct the zip-codes, as necessary
(*US Post Office*)
- New phone book every year!
(*Telecom USA*)
- Refuse collection – twice a week
(*Osceola County*)

It would be wrong, however, to paint too glowing a picture. Some aspects of the service were incredibly poor – for example, trying to get a problem resolved when the computer started rejecting my credit card, and trying to make use of telephone enquiries. Even getting through on the telephone to certain organizations is difficult – you are presented with a recorded message telling you to press button 3 for enquiries, button 4 for orders, button 5 for something else – and then whilst you wait you get a sales pitch for the organization.

All in all, I was impressed with the levels of service we received in America. With some exceptions, they have concentrated completely on getting both the attitudes and the systems improved to ensure a consistently high standard of service.

Part 5

SOME FINAL THOUGHTS

'What appears easy is often the most difficult.'

One of the fascinating things about top-rate professionals is that they make it look so easy. Years of experience, hard-work, constant practice and search for improvement can be distilled into momentary displays of virtuosity which are intensely satisfying to witness. We come to expect such 'excellent performance' from, the professional footballers, skaters, pop-singers and great actors of this world.

The obvious analogy is with customer service. It is rare that we enjoy virtuoso performances in any service delivery situation, yet when it occurs, it comes as a refreshing surprise. Often, such excellent customer service appears so easy and so natural, that we fail to understand why we do not receive it on a more regular basis.

In an increasingly competitive world, virtuoso customer service is virtually a mandatory aim for any incredibly successful business. Such virtuosity comes from the attainment of the highest standards together with constant innovation, constant striving for improvement and the development of trust and respect in all aspects of performance. In other words, virtuoso customer service requires a high degree of professionalism at all levels.

Managing to achieve *incredible customer service* is therefore all to do with the development and maintenance of a professional approach towards customers throughout the organization. Furthermore, to outclass the competition requires increasing degrees of virtuosity.

The 14 key tests of customer service outlined in Part 1 of this book reflect the essential standards for a professional approach to customer service. Any company which passes all these tests will indeed be exemplifying virtuoso customer service.

Such virtuosity can rarely be accomplished solely by prima donnas at the front-line. Even prima-donnas need coaching and support, together with sensitive and understanding management.

Superb people-management is therefore a crucial component in achieving superb customer service. Part 2 of this book concentrates on the key aspects of managing to achieve *incredible customer service*. Much of this focuses on achieving a positive attitude towards customer service, by developing a visionary people-oriented approach.

Another fascinating thing about customer service is that it is a critical aspect of your business which you can frequently improve instantly. Customer service has a simplicity and immediacy which many business school theorists find alien. It also has a certain implicit irrationality, in that those companies investing millions in customer service improvements often achieve less than those who do no more than motivate with an extra ounce of interest, together with an extra special smile. Part 3 of this book gives some examples of practical steps to be taken to achieve rapid improvements in customer service.

Finally, in Part 4, a broad cross-selection of case-studies are provided, of organizations that have sought to provide excellent customer service. In fact, through this book are scattered real-life stories customers tell about their experiences. One of the best ways to learn about customer service and how to improve it is to look at your own everyday life experiences.

There is nothing magical about achieving top-

rate customer service except that when you receive it it often appears 'magical'.

In the author's own company, 'Superboss', we are both fascinated by and obsessed with customer service. We want to learn continually and constantly seek to improve our approach. Sharing experiences about customer service with other people is a vital part of our ongoing process and applies not only in the work we do on training and management in customer service, or on customer service research, surveys and consultancy, but also in the way we deal with people on a day-by-day basis.

As a reader of this book, therefore, please do not hesitate to write to the author:

Dr David Freemantle
Chairman
Superboss Ltd
5 High Street
Windsor
Berkshire SL4 1LD
UK

He and his team will be delighted to hear from you and will do their best to give you a virtuoso response!